Withdrawn

What They Didn't Say

OXFORD
UNIVERSITY PRESS

Great Clarendon Street, Oxford OX2 6DP

Oxford University Press is a department of the University of Oxford.
It furthers the University's objective of excellence in research, scholarship,
and education by publishing worldwide in

Oxford New York

Auckland Cape Town Dar es Salaam Hong Kong Karachi Kuala Lumpur
Madrid Melbourne Mexico City Nairobi New Delhi Shanghai Taipei Toronto

With offices in

Argentina Austria Brazil Chile Czech Republic France Greece
Guatemala Hungary Italy Japan South Korea Poland Portugal
Singapore Switzerland Thailand Turkey Ukraine Vietnam

Oxford is a registered trade mark of Oxford University Press
in the UK and in certain other countries

Published in the United States
by Oxford University Press Inc., New York

British Library Cataloguing in Publication Data

Data available

Library of Congress Cataloging in Publication Data

Data available

Printed in Great Britain by
Clays Ltd, Bungay, Suffolk

ISBN: 0-19-920359-8
ISBN: 978-0-19-920359-8

1

What they Didn't Say

A BOOK OF MISQUOTATIONS

Edited by Elizabeth Knowles

OXFORD
UNIVERSITY PRESS

Contents

Introduction

Misquotations are often more than mistakes, and much more interesting. Many of them are quotations on the move, which are becoming part of our general vocabulary. We reach for them as a kind of shorthand through which we can make reference to a person, an event, or a particular situation. Thus the desire to evoke traditional conflicts of interest in the world of publishing may still lead someone to quote the popular form of Thomas Campbell's toast to Napoleon at a literary dinner: '**He once shot a publisher.**' Praise for a woman who has excelled in what has traditionally been seen as a man's world may be illuminated by reference to the comment attributed to Ginger Rogers—that she not only did everything her partner Fred Astaire did, but she did it '**backwards and in high heels**'. A reference to '**the white heat of technology**' may introduce comment on a strong belief in the effect of technological development.

The term 'misquotations' covers a range of quoted material: wrongly remembered sayings, where the incorrect version has established its own identity, popular summaries of original thoughts, and apocryphal or unverifiable comments attributed to a particular person. Some, like '**Beam me up, Scotty**', and '**Play it again, Sam**', are so well-known in their own right as to have achieved iconic status. Many of them represent unconscious editing by the memory, so that we refer to '**the best-laid plans o' mice and men**' rather than 'the best-laid schemes.' Charles Hoy Fort's 1931 comment, 'A social growth cannot find out the use of steam engines, until comes steam-engine time', is summarized and remembered as '**When it's steam engine time, people invent steam engines.**' (The critic Hesketh Pearson, considering this phenomenon in 1934, added in the idiom of his time: 'A widely-read man never quotes accurately, for the rather obvious reason that he has read too widely.')

Bernard Darwin, in his Introduction to the first edition of the *Oxford Dictionary of Quotations* in 1941, considered the uses to which the *Dictionary* might be put:

> It cannot accomplish impossibilities. It will not prevent many an honest journalist from referring to 'fresh fields and pastures new' nor from

describing a cup-tie as an example of 'Greek meeting Greek'. There is a fine old crusted tradition of misquoting not lightly to be broken and it might almost seem pedantry to deck these ancient friends in their true but unfamiliar colours. Misquoting may even be deemed an amiable weakness, since Dickens in one of his letters misquoted Sam Weller.

Darwin did go on to say that the *Dictionary* might offer 'a good chance of avoiding' the danger of misquotation, but the preceding passage suggests that he recognized the phenomenon of quotations which, in becoming part of the general vocabulary, adapt their form.

We adjust what we have heard, and sometimes build on the alteration. In J. D. Salinger's 1951 novel of adolescence, *The Catcher in the Rye*, the narrator Holden Caulfield relates his fantasy of a game played by children running through a field of rye near the edge of a cliff. He would like to be 'the catcher in the rye': the person who stands on the edge of the cliff, and catches them before they fall over. The fantasy is based on his mistaken memory of a song by Robert Burns. He explains it to his sister: 'You know that song "If a body catch a body comin' through the rye"? I'd like—'. She interrupts: 'It's "If a body *meet* a body coming through the rye"!' and continues, 'It's a poem. By Robert *Burns*.' Holden admits that she is right, but adds sadly 'I thought it was "If a body catch a body".' He is reluctant to relinquish either his fantasy, or the changed wording on which it was based.

We may unconsciously edit what we remember to fit what we believe to be the essential truth about a person or an event. The misquotation then flourishes because it echoes more precisely a common assumption, or encapsulates the public profile of a particular person. A written source may confirm 'the opposition of events' as Harold Macmillan's view of the greatest difficulty for a Prime Minister, but 'Events, dear boy. Events' catches the tone of that political personality. The supposed assertion 'You've never had it so good' fits with the image of 'Supermac' as successful Premier. The insouciant 'I rob banks because that's where the money is' evokes the public persona of the debonair American bank robber Willie Sutton, known as 'the Actor'. 'If I can't dance, I don't want to be in your revolution', as addressed to a puritanical comrade, has the sparky feel of the revolutionary Emma Goldman. The ominous statement 'The Republic has no need of scientists' catches the icy tone of the Jacobins at the time of the Terror. The injunction 'Pray for Shackleton' (from the longer 'When disaster strikes, get down on your knees and pray for Shackleton'), reflects the reputation for competence and effectiveness of the Antarctic explorer Ernest Shackleton. Occasionally this has presented problems: Winston Churchill's choice of epithets for his Labour opponent Clement Attlee included 'a sheep in sheep's clothing' and 'a modest man with much to be modest about', but he deplored the suggestion that he might have said 'An empty taxi drew up outside 10 Downing Street, and Attlee got out.'

A small change may reflect a real difference in meaning. 'Advise, encourage, and warn' is frequently given as the right of a sovereign: in this version, the active verb 'to advise' has replaced the passive 'to be consulted' which appeared in Bagehot's original text. 'A democracy, if you can keep it', as attributed to Benjamin Franklin, reflects concerns of the contemporary world more nearly than the 'republic' (wrested from the control of a monarchical state) of which Franklin actually spoke.

It is, of course, always possible that the 'popular' version, rather than the official record, represents what was actually said. The process is shown, neatly, in a fictional source. In 1981, Jonathan Lynn and Antony Jay published the first volume of *Yes Minister: the diaries of a Cabinet Minister*, based on their successful television series. In the first chapter, the hapless Hacker reproduces an extract from *Hansard*, giving the 'amusing question' which he had asked the previous year. The extract concludes 'Opposition laughter, and government cries of "shame".' An editorial note below records: 'Actually they cried "Bollocks" Ed.' The question of whether the official record necessarily reports exactly what was said comes up with 'Speak for England' (or 'Britain') as said by Leo Amery or Robert Boothby in the House of Commons in 1941. It is also relevant when considering whether Ernest Bevin accused George Lansbury of 'hawking', 'taking', or indeed 'carting' his conscience round at the Labour Conference in 1935.

Sometimes, frustratingly, it is possible to find contemporary evidence of a train of thought which is later summarized in a popular attribution. It is possible to find a passage of direct quotation from Napoleon in which the ex-Emperor summed up the dangers of attacking China ('You would teach them their own strength'). There does not, unfortunately, appear to be any contemporary support for the later, more colourful warning: '**China is a sleeping giant. But when she wakes, the world will tremble.**'

In a few cases, the amended version may be the work of the original speaker. The archaeologist Howard Carter's notebook for November 1922 records what happened when he first looked into the tomb of Tutankhamun. Lord Carnarvon, presumably watching anxiously, asked if he could see anything, to which Carter apparently replied 'Yes, it is wonderful.' But in the written-up account published some years later, Carter improves on the wording, and gives as his response, '**Yes, wonderful things.**'

A misquotation which is partly or wholly fictional may be damaging to the person to whom it is attributed. The challenge of the nineteenth-century Tammany leader 'Boss' Tweed, '**What are you going to do about it?**', may have originated as a hostile cartoon caption, but it fitted exactly the public perception of arrogant Tammany confidence in its corrupt empire, and contributed to Tweed's downfall. From an earlier period, the belief that Marie Antoinette said '**Let them eat cake**' contributed lastingly to the hostile picture of a frivolous and selfish queen far removed from her subjects.

Misquotations may represent a conversation between two people, so that a single sentence is attributed to one (usually famous) speaker. When the Prince of Wales announced his engagement to Lady Diana Spencer in 1981, he was asked by a journalist if he were 'in love'. His reply was, 'Yes...whatever that may mean.' The troubled history of their marriage undoubtedly helped establish what became the popular version of his words: '**Whatever "in love" means.**' A storm of protest greeted the reports in 1999 that the Prime Minister of Australia, John Howard, had suggested that Australia as an Asia-Pacific power would act '**deputy sheriff in the region**' to the United States. In the original interview, John Howard had listened to a journalist's question as to whether he saw Australia's role as America's deputy, and had filled in the words 'in the region'. He then had to deny subsequent reports which attributed the full, and much more definite, description to him.

Some misquotations will generate phrases—such as '**gilding the lily**'—which become entirely detached from the original source. Others, like '**He who hesitates is lost**', move into the area of proverbial wisdom: again, the original formulation is increasingly distant. A notable (and appropriate) example of this is the terse adjuration '**Always verify your references.**' The original form in which we have the advice of the classicist Dr Routh is: 'You will find it a very good practice always to verify your references, sir!' Many misquotations, however, remain linked to a person or an event, and the change they display illuminates the way in which that person or event is perceived in the public mind.

Misattributions often derive from the tendency to attach a well-known saying to a well-known name: as Dorothy Parker pointed out, '**We all assume that Oscar [Wilde] said it.**' In some cases, the saying belongs in a particular world, but is subsequently attached to a later figure from that world. The question '**Why is this lying bastard lying to me?**', supposedly one which the British journalist Jeremy Paxman asks himself before embarking on an interview, can be traced back via an earlier journalist, Louis Heren of the *Times*, to advice given to Heren by an unnamed correspondent of the *Daily Worker* in the mid 1940s. The dates and people involved change: the skepticism of a journalist encountering an 'official source' is constant. Other famous lines which can be traced back to an earlier coinage are likely to represent a conscious (and affectionate) borrowing, as in Ronald Reagan's rueful '**I forgot to duck**', from the boxer Jack Dempsey. Some items begin as borrowings and are then reworked: Stanley Baldwin borrowed '**Power without responsibility**' from his cousin Rudyard Kipling. Many years later Tom Stoppard reworked it as '**Responsibility without power**'.

Most of the misquotations considered above related to alterations made through a process of language change. They conform to Hesketh Pearson's view that 'Misquotations belong to the people, not poets.' However, misquotation may be used as a deliberate literary (and indeed poetic) device. A reworking may contain a conscious allusion to a significant original. T. S. Eliot borrowed, and changed from the third to the first person, words from the seventeenth-century sermons of Lancelot Andrewes for the opening line of his poem on the Magi's Christmas journey, '**A cold coming we had of it**.' The concluding words of W. H. Auden's poem 'Epitaph on a Tyrant' (1940) are '**When he cried the little children died in the streets**.' Not only did this evoke powerfully the image of a ruthless dictator, it implicitly contrasted the description of a tyrant with a famous nineteenth-century comment on a much more admirable ruler. The American historian John Lothrop Motley, writing in 1856 about the Protestant hero William of Orange, 'the Silent', founding father of the Dutch Republic, said of him, 'As long as he lived, he was the guiding-star of a whole brave nation, and when he died the little children cried in the streets.'

Sometimes the element taken is part of a longer phrase: this happens frequently with book titles taken from the work of an earlier author. Hardy borrowed the title of his 1874 novel *Far From the Madding Crowd* from a line in Gray's *Elegy Written in a Country Churchyard* (1751), '**Far from the madding crowd's ignoble strife**'. At other times the structure of the borrowed phrase is adjusted, so that it can stand by itself without losing its allusive force. William Faulkner's *The Sound and the Fury* (1929) thus recalls its source: the bleak view of life given in Shakespeare's *Macbeth* (1606):

> It is a tale
> Told by an idiot, full of sound and fury,
> Signifying nothing.

T. E. Lawrence's *The Seven Pillars of Wisdom* (1926) has moved further still from the book of *Proverbs* in the Authorized Version of the Bible (1611): 'Wisdom hath builded her house, she hath hewn out her seven pillars.'

Misquotation or misattribution can be used in fictional surroundings to suggest character. In Jane Austen's *Emma*, the affected Mrs Elton slightly misquotes Gray's *Elegy Written in a Country Churchyard*, insisting that Jane Fairfax should not be allowed to 'blush unseen', and waste her 'fragrance' (rather than her 'sweetness') 'on the desert air'. It seems quite probable that the inaccuracy is intended to give the reader a sense of the superficiality of Mrs. Elton's self-proclaimed culture.

Allan Quartermain, the narrator of Rider Haggard's novel *King Solomon's Mines*, describing a battle, quotes a passage from Walter Scott's account of the Battle of Flodden Field in the poem *Marmion*:

> The stubborn spearmen still made good
> The dark impenetrable wood;
> Each stepping where his comrade stood
> The instant that he fell.

He adds as reference 'as I think the "Ingoldsby Legends" beautifully puts it'. Robert Louis Stevenson pointed out to Haggard that he had awarded Scott's lines to the clergyman and humorous writer Richard Harris Barham (1788–1845). He was told in reply that Allan Quartermain's habit of attributing various quotations to the only two works of literature he knew, the Old Testament and *The Ingoldsby Legends*, was a 'literary joke'. It was also presumably part of the characterization of the man of action, 'Hunter' Quartermain.

Other 'misquotations' really represent variant readings. '**Richard's himself again**', as spoken by Lawrence Olivier as Richard III in his film of Shakespeare's play, is a line added in the 18th century by the dramatist Colley Cibber. *Hamlet* is one of the longest Shakespearian plays, and truncated versions include one from which the character of Horatio has been excised. Mark Lawson has suggested that those who first said '**Alas, poor Yorick. I knew him well**' rather than 'Alas, poor Yorick. I knew him, Horatio' may have recalled the line from a performance of such a text.

With one category of misquotation, it is the structure of the original that remains constant, giving rise to a wide number of variants rather than to a single changed form. Elements within the essential framework change to suit the given circumstances. In Oscar Wilde's *The Importance of Being Ernest*, Lady Bracknell declaims, 'To lose one parent, Mr Worthing, may be regarded as a misfortune; to lose both looks like carelessness.' The formulation 'to lose one...to lose both' as a way of indicating a progressive deterioration is now part of the common lexicon. A report on France's exit from the 2002 World Cup, having lost key players Zinedine Zidane and Robert Pires to injury, concluded: 'To lose one of your two best players could be considered unfortunate; to lose both is a disaster.'

In 1993, Tony Blair told his Party Conference that 'Labour is the party of law and order in Britain today. Tough on crime and tough on the causes of crime.' In 1996, considerable publicity attended the news that a member of the Labour Shadow Front Bench, Harriet Harman, had chosen to send her son to a fee-paying school. In a House of Commons exchange, the then Prime Minister, John Major, chose to rework his opponent's sound bite in the light of this story, claiming that he wanted to be 'tough on hypocrisy, and tough on the causes of hypocrisy.' It is the form of the original quotation ('tough on...and tough on the cause of...'), rather than the precise words, which has embedded itself in the language. Because of their structure, the original 'to lose one parent...' and 'tough on crime, and tough on the causes of crime' formulations are capable of wide variety while remaining recognizable, and traceable back to the original text.

It is tempting to think of misquotations which are now familiar to us as having taken time to establish themselves, but a recent example shows how quickly an erroneous wording can take root. In the aftermath of 9/11, a leaked email sent by Jo Moore, a British government adviser, became the subject of heated comment in the British press. It was reported that during the afternoon of 11 September 2001, Miss Moore had sent an email suggesting that it would be a good moment to make public anything that it was hoped would escape notice as this would be '**a good day to bury bad news**'. In fact, her email, as reported in the *Daily Telegraph* of 10 October 2001, had read 'It is now a very good day to get out anything we want to bury', but it is the pithier summary of her advice which has added itself to the language.

It is a (perhaps predictable) feature of established misquotations that they are associated with a high level of public recognition. Sometimes, as with '**the green shoots of recovery**', the popular version of the statement by Norman Lamont, as Chancellor, that 'The green shoots of economic spring are emerging once again', the original is a much-reported comment. At other times, the misquotation reflects an erroneous understanding of what is seen as a characteristic saying. One notable example of this is '**Elementary, my dear Watson**', as attributed to Conan Doyle's detective Sherlock Holmes. In fact, the nearest Holmes comes to it is in this exchange with Dr Watson: ' "Excellent," I cried. "Elementary," said he.' The first instance of the familiar form is found nearly 30 years later, in a novel by P. G. Wodehouse: '"Elementary, my dear Watson, elementary," murmured Psmith.'

In this case, the misquotation enshrines what is seen as part of the essential relation between the brilliant Holmes and the slower Watson. Similarly, '**Beam me up, Scotty**' is supposedly the form in which Captain Kirk habitually requested to be returned from a planet to the Starship *Enterprise*. In fact, the nearest equivalent found is 'Beam us up, Mr. Scott' in the episode 'Gamesters of Triskelion'.

The process of reducing a sentence to a phrase which summarizes the central idea is a standard way for 'misquotations' to work. At times, the compressed version represents conscious choice by the speaker: it is a neat way of alluding to a known, but much longer, original. In April 2004 Condoleezza Rice, then United States National Security Advisor, said in an interview, '**When the Founding Fathers said "we the people", they did not mean me. My ancestors were three-fifths of a man.**' Dr Rice was alluding to the Constitution of the United States (1787). The preamble opened, 'We the people of the United States'. Article 1 of the Constitution, setting out its choice of the electorate, continued:

> Representatives and direct taxes shall be apportioned among the several States which may be included within this Union, according to their respective numbers, which shall be determined by adding to the whole number of free persons, including those bound to service for a term of years, and excluding Indians not taxed, three fifths of all other persons.

The phrase 'selling the family silver' to indicate the willingness to dispose of or compromise goods or values which should be treasured is now established in the language, and is often referred back to Harold Macmillan. However, in his speech criticizing the actions of Margaret Thatcher's government on privatization, what he said was: 'First of all the Georgian silver goes, and then all that nice furniture that used to be in the saloon. Then the Canalettos go.' '**Selling the family silver**' was understood as the gist of what Macmillan was saying; it is also the form in which his words are now quoted.

Summaries of this kind are likely to establish themselves in the language without being attributable to a particular person; they

simply become the preferred form for anyone who wishes to allude
to the quotation, as if by a general consensus. Occasionally, however,
we do know the origin of the misquotation. 'Crisis? What Crisis?',
still sometimes attributed directly to James Callaghan, was a famous
Sun newspaper headline which was deeply damaging to the then
Prime Minister.

Apocryphal quotations may be created as reflecting a
particular persona. Sam Goldwyn was not responsible for all the
'Goldwynisms' freely quoted today. Although Dr Spooner did turn
'the rate of wages' as a pressure on the employer into 'the weight of
rages', it is sadly unlikely that he told an errant undergraduate that
'**You have deliberately tasted two whole worms and you can leave
Oxford by the town drain.**' In our own time, George W. Bush cannot
safely be credited with all the 'Bushisms' that are widely circulated.
Noël Coward clearly understood the process when he wrote in his
diary for 19 March 1955:

> The only thing that really saddens me over my demise is that I shall not
> be here to read the nonsense that will be written about me...There will
> be lists of apocryphal jokes I never made and gleeful misquotations of
> words I never said. *What* a pity I shan't be here to enjoy them!

Quotations, true or false, may contribute materially to shaping
the public's view of a particular person. Where politicians are
concerned it is interesting to reflect for a moment on the role of the
speechwriter. Margaret Thatcher famously told her Party Conference
in 1980: 'To those waiting with baited breath for that favourite
media catch-phrase, the U-turn, I have only this to say. 'You turn
if you want; the lady's not for turning.' This reworking of the title
of Christopher Fry's 1949 play *The Lady's not for Burning* is probably
now one of Margaret Thatcher's best-known quotations, but it was
actually written for her by her speechwriter Ronald Millar. (In his
memoirs, Millar noted of '**the lady's not for turning**'—TLNFT as he
referred to it—that he was unsure whether the original title would
still be remembered in 1980, or if it mattered.)

Peggy Noonan, speechwriter from the later era of Ronald Reagan,
has given an account of writing the text of the presidential broadcast
on the loss of the space shuttle *Challenger* and its crew, from which
one of the best-remembered 'Reagan quotations' comes: 'We will

never forget them, nor the last time we saw them this morning, as they prepared for the journey and waved goodbye and "slipped the surly bonds of earth" to "touch the face of God".

In January 1986, the *Challenger*, with its seven crew members, was destroyed just after lift-off. Many watching the broadcast of the launch had been schoolchildren, as one of the crew was a teacher, who had planned to give a lesson from space. It was immediately clear that the President would need to make an address to the American people. In her memoir *What I Saw at the Revolution* (1990), Peggy Noonan describes writing it, and feeling unsure before the delivery that the words would be equal to the occasion. But the broadcast was warmly received. The following month *Time Magazine*, under the heading 'They slipped the surly bonds of earth to touch the face of God' noted that: 'President Reagan, in a moving broadcast to the nation that afternoon, paraphrased a sonnet written by John Gillespie Magee, a young American airman killed in World War II.' Magee, who was killed while flying with the Royal Canadian Airforce, had written:

> Oh! I have slipped the surly bonds of earth
> And danced the skies on laughter-silvered wings...
> And, while with silent lifting mind I've trod
> The high, untrespassed sanctity of space,
> Put out my hand and touched the face of God.

Peggy Noonan had deftly brought together two phrases from the poem to create the line for which Ronald Reagan would be remembered. Ironically, by her own account, she had to fight off a staffer's attempt to change 'touch the face of God' to 'reach out and touch someone—touch the face of God', on the grounds that this would be more eloquent.

It is of course quite possible to point to misquotations which are verbal slips—and which do not necessarily leave their mark. The poet and classicist A. E. Housman, known for his textual rigour, reported ruefully, in a letter of December 1927, that he had been visited by the famous American defence attorney, Clarence Darrow. Darrow had come out of retirement, in 1924, to defend the young killers Leopold and Loeb. His powerful plea for mitigation (through which the death sentence had been avoided) included quotations from

Housman's poetry. Housman wrote to his brother of the meeting:

> He had only a few days in England, but he could not return home
> without seeing me, because he had so often used my poems to rescue his
> clients from the electric chair. Loeb and Leopold owe their life sentence
> partly to me; and he gave me a copy of his speech, in which, sure enough,
> two of my pieces are misquoted.

Some verbal slips, of course, can have a lasting impact. '**Facts are
stupid things**' (for 'Facts are stubborn things' by John Adams) was a
momentary error of Ronald Reagan's, instantly corrected, but it is
still widely quoted and remembered.

It has to be admitted that (understandably) misquotation has
had a bad press. The aspiring writer in Byron's *English Bards and
Scotch Reviewers* was envisaged as having 'just enough of learning
to misquote'. The American writer Washington Irving, in *Tales of
a Traveller*, published in 1824 as by 'Geoffrey Crayon, gent.' does
describe a situation in which an author accepts being misquoted,
but the circumstances are not particularly creditable. The narrator
has met an enthusiastic (and vocal) admirer of his own work:

> Every now and then he would break out with some scrap which he would
> misquote most terribly, but would rub his hands and exclaim, 'By Jupiter
> that's fine! That's noble! Damme, sir, if I can conceive how you hit upon
> such ideas!'
>   I must confess I did not always relish his misquotations, which
> sometimes made absolute nonsense of the passages; but what author
> stands upon trifles when he is praised?

But while it is always of interest to trace the origin of a familiar
saying, a changed form that establishes itself in the language has
its own reality, and tells us something of interest about our own
perceptions. And if all else fails, refuge from pedantic correction can
be found in the person of Thomas Carlyle. The poet Robert Graves,
in his memoir *Good-bye to All That*, recalled pointing out to the
critic Augustine Birrell that Elihu was not the name of one of Job's
comforters. Birrell responded: 'I will say to you what Thomas Carlyle
once said to a young man who caught him out in a misquotation:
"Young man, you are heading straight for the pit of hell!"'

The misquotations in this book are arranged in a single A–Z

sequence (with 'a' and 'the' being ignored). A full list of items covered is found on p. xviii. An index of the names of those mentioned in the individual entries, with direction to the entry concerned, is found on p. 141.

To compile this book I have drawn on the resources of Oxford Quotations Dictionaries: our published texts and our growing database of new quotations derived from our reading programme. My colleague James McCracken of Oxford English Dictionaries generously, and crucially, shared his expertise to allow us to benefit from evidence provided by the Oxford English Corpus. I am grateful to all those who have contributed to the identification and verification of the background of particular items, especially Ralph Bates, Susanne Charlett, Jean Harker, and Verity Mason. Peter Kemp and Fiona Stafford gave illuminating advice on the shaping of the project. Penny Trumble was a meticulous proof-reader. As always, the key support and advice of one who is herself an expert Quotations editor has been provided by Susan Ratcliffe.

It is said that 'Of making many books, there is no end': this is self-evidently true of the making of misquotations. There is always one more to be found: not just to correct it to its original form, but to see the way in which it is being adapted and used. The misquotations examined in this book are a selection, chosen partly because of the evidence for their life in the language, and partly to show the liveliness and diversity of this particular form. It has been enormously enjoyable to work on the book: I hope I have been able to share some of the pleasure and interest I have felt with our readers.

Elizabeth Knowles
Oxford, March 2006

Misquotations

Actors are cattle
Adding a new terror to life
Advise, encourage, and warn
Alas, poor Yorick
All human life is there
All is lost save honour
All rowed fast, but none so fast as stroke
All we have done is awaken a sleeping giant
Always something new out of Africa
Ask not what your country can do for you
As Maine goes, so goes Vermont

Backing into the limelight
Backwards and in high heels
Bad money drives out good
The ballot is stronger than the bullet
The battle of Waterloo was won on the playing fields of Eton
Beam me up, Scotty
A beginning, a muddle, and an end
The best-laid plans of mice and men
Books do furnish a room
The British are coming!
The budget should be balanced...
Build a better mousetrap

The capitalists will sell us the rope with which to hang them
A chicken in every pot
A child is not a vase to be filled, but a fire to be lit
City of dreaming spires
A cold coming we had of it
Come with me to the Casbah
Comment is free, but facts are on expenses
Consistency is the hobgoblin of little minds
A contemptible little army

Corporations have neither bodies to be punished nor souls to be damned
A covenant with death, and an agreement with hell
Crisis? What Crisis?
Culture is the best which has been thought and said

Dark forces at work
Dark night of the soul
The decent obscurity of a learned language
A democracy, if you can keep it
Deputy sheriff in the region
Dissent is the highest form of patriotism
Don't unchain the tiger
Do what thou wilt shall be the whole of the law
Dreams are the royal road to the unconscious
The dwarf sees farther than the giant

Economical with the truth
Elementary, my dear Watson
An empty taxi
Engineers of the soul
England and America are two countries divided by a common language
The English are a nation of shopkeepers
The even tenor of one's way
Events, dear boy. Events

Facts are stupid things
Failure is not an option
Fate knocking at the door
A feather on the breath of God
Fellow immigrants
Few die and none resign
Fiery the angels fell
First catch your hare
The fog of war

Follow the money
Frankly, my dear, I don't give a damn!
Fresh fields and pastures new
The future is plastics

Genius is an infinite capacity for taking pains
Germany is my spiritual home
Gild the lily
Git thar fustest with the mostest
God does not play dice
Gold is a barbarous relic
The good Christian should beware of mathematicians
A good day to bury bad news
Go west, young man
Greater love hath no man than this, that he lay down his friends for his life
The green shoots of recovery
Gunpowder, printing, and the Protestant religion

Hamlet without the Prince
Happiness is a warm —
Hawking his conscience round the Chancelleries of Europe
A heartbeat away from the Presidency
Hell hath no fury like a woman scorned
He once shot a publisher
He snatched the lightning shaft from heaven
He who hesitates is lost
Hold the fort! I am coming!
Homer sometimes nods
An honest God is the noblest work of man
A hundred guilty witches

I am become Death, the destroyer of worlds
I am *the* American
I disapprove of what you say, but I will defend to the death your right to say it

I don't know what effect these men will have upon the enemy, but, by God, they frighten me
If I can't dance, I don't want to be in your revolution
I forgot to duck
If the glove doesn't fit, you must acquit
If we are not for ourselves, then who will be with us?
If you build it, they will come
If you cannot measure it, then it is not science
If you can't ride two horses at once, you shouldn't be in the circus
If you haven't got anything good to say about anyone come and sit by me
I had hoped that liberal and enlightened thought would have reconciled the Christians
I have gazed upon the face of Agamemnon
I never loved a dear gazelle
An inn where all are received
An inordinate fondness for beetles
Instead of rocking the cradle, they rocked the system
In trust I have found treason
I rob banks because that's where the money is
Is that a pistol in your pocket, or are you just glad to see me?
It is impossible to rightly govern the world without God and the Bible
It is necessary only for the good man to do nothing for evil to triumph
It's a funny old world
It's life, Jim, but not as we know it
It's not the voting that's democracy, it's the counting
I used to be the next President
I want to be alone

Justice delayed is justice denied
Justify the ways of God to man

Misquotations

The lady's not for turning
Laws are like sausages
Lead on, Macduff
The leopard does not change his spots
Let the boy win his spurs
Let them eat cake
A lie is an abomination unto the Lord
Life is not meant to be easy
A little knowledge is a dangerous thing
Look out, gentlemen—the schoolmaster
is abroad!

Make the trains run on time
Man, if you gotta ask, you'll never know
Man's love is of man's life a thing apart
Me Tarzan, you Jane
Mind has no sex
Monkeys on typewriters
The most beautiful adventure
The Mother of Parliaments
Mr Balfour's poodle
My lips are sealed

Natural selection is a mechanism for
generating an exceedingly high degree of
improbability
Nice guys finish last
A noble experiment
Nobody ever lost money by underrating
public taste
No plan survives first contact with the
enemy
Nothing to lose but your yolks
Not tonight, Josephine
Now Barabbas was a publisher

O Diamond! Diamond!
Old maids bicycling to Holy
Communion
Once aboard the lugger and the maid is
mine
One indissoluble bond
One small step for man
Outside every fat man

The past is not dead
Peace for our time
Pennies don't fall from heaven
Play it again, Sam
Play the — card
Politics is the art of the impossible
The pound in your pocket
Power corrupts
Praise from Sir Hubert is praise indeed
Pray for Shackleton
Pride goes before a fall
The proper study of mankind is books
Put me back on my bike

Rather light a candle than curse the
darkness
Rearrange the deckchairs on the Titanic
Rejoice, rejoice
Religion is the foundation of
government
Reports of my death have been greatly
exaggerated
The Republic has no need of scientists
Responsibility without power
Revealed religion has no weight with me
Rivers of blood
Rum, sodomy, and the lash
The Rupert of Debate

Safety in numbers
Save the gerund, and screw the whale
See how these Christians love one
another
Selling off the family silver
Shaken, not stirred
Shouting fire in a crowded theatre
The sick man of —
Sketch the ruins of St Paul's
Slipped the surly bonds of earth to touch
the face of God
Small earthquake in Chile
The soft underbelly of Europe
Some men are born mediocre
Some of the jam we thought was for
tomorrow, we've already eaten

Something must be done
The South is avenged
Speak for England
Spend less time with one's family
Squeeze Germany till the pips squeak
A straight sort of guy

Take away these baubles
Tectonic plates
Tell your kids to get their scooters off my lawn
That fable of Christ
Theories pass. The frog remains
There but for the grace of God go I
A thing of beauty and a boy forever
A thing of shreds and patches
The thin red line
Three bodies no sensible man challenges
Three-fifths of a man
Throw another shrimp on the barbie
The time was out of joint
To err is human, but to really foul things up requires a computer
To the Puritan all things are impure
Treason is a matter of dates
The triple cord
Trip the light fantastic
The truth which makes one free
Two wise acres and a cow

Up like a rocket, down like a stick

Variety is the spice of life
The voice we heard was that of Mr Churchill
Vox populi, vox humbug

War is the continuation of politics by other means
The war to end war
Warts and all
Was für plundern!
Watch what we do, not what we say
We are the masters now
A week is a long time in politics

A wee pretendy Parliament
We have met the enemy, and he is us
We must educate our masters
We trained hard...
What a glorious morning for America
What are you going to do about it?
Whatever 'in love' means
What the soldier said isn't evidence
Whenever I hear the word culture, I reach for my pistol
When Greek meets Greek, then comes the tug of war
When he cried the little children died in the streets
When in Rome, do as the Romans do
When it's steam engine time, people invent steam engines
When the legend becomes fact, print the legend
Where every prospect pleases
Where's the beef?
While there is death there is hope
A white glove pulpit
The white heat of technology
Who breaks a butterfly on a wheel?
Whom the gods wish to destroy they first call promising
Whose woods these are everybody knows exactly
Why don't you come up and see me sometime?
Why is this lying bastard lying to me?
Will it play in Peoria?
Winning isn't everything
Winter of discontent

Yes, wonderful things
You cannot strengthen the weak by weakening the strong
You dirty rat!
You have deliberately tasted two whole worms
You've never had it so good

Actors are cattle

This dismissive statement was attributed to the film director Alfred Hitchcock in the *Saturday Evening Post* for 22 May 1943, although according to a later source, 'Hitch' afterwards qualified the remark by asserting, '**What I said was, actors should be *treated* like cattle.**' The shorter form, however, became part of the Hitchcock legend. According to one anecdote, during the filming of *Mr and Mrs Smith* (1941), the actress Carole Lombard had three calves brought on to the set before filming began for the day. All three had labels tied round their necks, reading respectively 'Carole Lombard', Robert Montgomery, and 'Gene Raymond', the names of the three stars of the film.

Adding a new terror to life

The actor-manager Herbert Beerbohm Tree, asked by a gramophone company to endorse their product, is said to have responded with the message: '**Sirs, I have tested your machine. It adds a new terror to life and makes death a long-felt want.**' The expression has been used in other contexts: in August 2005 the novelist Hilary Mantel commented that '**In recent years the publication of the Booker long list has added a new terror to life.**'

According to a phrase established earlier in the literary world, the threat of a bad biography could also 'add a new terror to death'. (It was presumably in this spirit that the novelist William Thackeray adjured his daughters, 'Mind, no biography!') The expression is found in verdicts on the *Lives of the Lord Chancellors*, published between 1845 and 1847 by a former Lord Chancellor, Lord Campbell. His contemporary Lord St Leonards, in his 1869 *Misrepresentations in Campbell's Lives of Lyndhurst and Brougham*, recounted how, at a dinner at which he himself was present, Sir Charles Wetherell had addressed Lord Campbell: '**Then there is my noble and biographical friend who has added a new terror to death.**' Lord St Leonards continued:

I have lived to find that he has left behind him a new terror to life. After such a publication as the Lives of Lord Lyndhurst and Lord Brougham, no man can be sure that he may not be libelled and misrepresented by an attack published in his lifetime.

An associated image is found still earlier in a letter written to Jonathan Swift by the Scottish physician and pamphleteer John Arbuthnot, about the activities of the bookseller (and publisher) Edmund Curll. In the verse in which he looked forward to the public reaction to his own death, Swift had summed up his view of Curll:

He'll treat me as he does my betters.
Publish my will, my life, my letters.
Revive the libels born to die;
Which Pope must bear, as well as I.
(Verses on the Death of Dr Swift, 1731.)

In 1733, Arbuthnot wrote to Swift: '**Curll (who is one of the new terrors of death) has been writing letters to every body for memoirs of his life.**'

Advise, encourage, and warn

These words (occasionally with the order of the first two reversed) are often used to summarize the role of a constitutional monarch. In the *Observer* of 26 February 2006, discussing the role of the sovereign in the context of debate over the Prince of Wales, Robert Hazell, director of the Constitution Unit at the London School of Economics, said:

Prince Charles is not the monarch...The key is how he behaves once he is king. He then does have formal powers to encourage, to advise and to warn and he has an opportunity once a week to do so.

The source of what has become an established phrase is *The English Constitution* (1867) by the political commentator and economist Walter Bagehot. However, Bagehot's original formulation differed slightly. The passage reads: '**The Sovereign has, under a** constitutional monarchy such as ours, three rights—the right to be consulted, the right to encourage, the right to warn.' In the popular summary, the passive 'to be consulted' has been replaced by the active 'to advise'.

Alas, poor Yorick

Hamlet's lament in the graveyard near Elsinore, standing over the grave of the jester Yorick, is often quoted as '**Alas, poor Yorick. I knew him well.**' In her 2000 memoir *Bad Blood*, the critic and novelist Lorna Sage wrote evocatively of the clerical grandfather who was a dominant figure of her childhood. In the first chapter, she described a scene in which she and her grandfather saw the gravedigger, at work, unearthing a skull in the old churchyard. Her grandfather picked up the skull, 'dusted off the soil and declaimed: "Alas, poor Yorick, I knew him well"'.

> '**Alas poor Yorick. I knew him well**'

The textually correct reading is actually 'Alas, poor Yorick. I knew him, Horatio.' However, 'I knew him well' may not be simply a failure of memory. It has been pointed out that in some heavily cut versions of *Hamlet*, the character of Horatio was excised. 'I knew him well' could have derived from the memory of a performance of one of these.

All human life is there

A slogan for the *News of the World* newspaper in the late 1950s, coined by the then Editor, Maurice Smelt. As recalled by the writer Fay Weldon in her memoir *Auto da Fay* (2002), '**He it was who invented the slogan '*All Human Life is There*' for the *News of the World*, or at least retrieved it from Henry James.**'

As used by the *News of the World*, the slogan was a positive one, but in Henry James's *The Madonna of the Future* (1879) the connotations were somewhat different. A model-maker is displaying the plastic figurines that he has made:

What do you say to my types, signore? The idea is bold; does it strike you as happy? Cats and monkeys—monkeys and cats—all human life is there! Human life, of course, I mean, viewed with the eye of the satirist! To combine sculpture and satire, signore, has been my unprecedented ambition. I flatter myself that I have not egregiously failed.

All is lost save honour

In 1525, the army of Francis I of France was defeated in battle at Pavia, and the king himself captured, by the forces of the Emperor Charles V. Francis subsequently wrote to his mother, Louise of Savoy: '*De toutes choses ne m'est demeuré que l'honneur et la vie quie est saulve* [Of all I had, only honour and life have been spared].'

The letter was published in French in a collection of historical documents in 1847, but the shorter version is to be found in English earlier in the century, as in the following extract from Frances Thurtle Jamieson's *A History of France*, published in 1818: 'It was after this decisive blow that Francis wrote the justly celebrated Spartan letter to his mother, containing the following words only: "Madam, all is lost, save Honour."'

All rowed fast, but none so fast as stroke

A would-be but nonsensical endorsement of a successful rowing crew which (as the 1953 second edition of the *Oxford Dictionary of Quotations* noted) has often been attributed to that flamboyant figure of the Victorian and Edwardian worlds, the novelist Ouida. This is possibly unsurprising: as the critic Bonamy Dobrée noted in an appreciative article published in the *Listener* in 1932, she had a reputation for what had been called 'diverting inaccuracies'.

In fact, it derives from a much longer passage in a comic novel of Oxford life, Desmond Coke's *Sandford of Merton* (1903):

His blade struck the water a full second before any other: the lad had started well. Nor did he flag as the race wore on...as the boats began to near the winning-post, his oar was dipping into the water nearly *twice* as often as any other.

On the title page of *Sandford of Merton*, Desmond Coke is given as the editor. The authorship is credited to 'Miss Belinda Blinders', who is further said to have provided 'a clever view of Oxford and her ways'. It seems highly possible that a confusion with the fictional Miss Blinders explains the attribution to the real Ouida.

All we have done is awaken a sleeping giant

Supposedly said by Admiral Isoruko Yamamoto (1884–1943), who as Japanese Commander-in-Chief was responsible for planning the 1941 attack on Pearl Harbor. In the 1970 film *Tora! Tora! Tora!*, his character is given the lines, '**I fear we have only awakened a sleeping giant, and his reaction will be terrible.**'

There is no evidence that Yamamoto used these words, and in a letter of 9 January 1942 he wrote: '**A military man can scarcely pride himself on having "smitten a sleeping enemy"; in fact, to have it pointed out is more a matter of shame.**'

The image of a powerful country as a sleeping giant roused to dangerous anger by attack is now a familiar one. In *Safire's New Political Dictionary* (1993), William Safire records a 1978 reference from the *Wall Street Journal* in which the comment '**China is a sickly, sleeping giant. But when she awakes the world will tremble**' is attributed to Napoleon. In 2006, an online search for 'China is a sleeping giant' together with 'Napoleon' returned hundreds of hits. However, to trace any of these references back to an earlier source is much harder.

Barry O'Meara, who for a time was Napoleon's personal surgeon on St Helena, recorded a number of conversations with the ex-Emperor in his book, *Napoleon in Exile*, published in 1822. In 1817, Lord Amherst, who had led a diplomatic mission to China, visited St Helena, and this brought the topic of China to Napoleon's mind. He gave a vivid picture of the dangers of going to war with China, even if at first the attack were successful: 'You would teach them their own strength. They would be compelled to adopt measures to defend themselves against you.' In the end they would get technical help 'from France and America, and even from London; they would build a fleet, and, in the course of time, defeat you'.

The essential idea is here, if not, frustratingly, the figure of speech. It does however make it understandable that the more dramatic version should now be put into Napoleon's mouth.

Always something new out of Africa

A proverbial expression, translating the Latin *ex Africa semper aliquid novi*, used in English from the mid sixteenth century; since 1937, the phrase has probably also evoked the thought of Karen Blixen's memoir *Out of Africa*. In June 2000, a report appeared on the CBS News website with the title 'Out of Africa: Elephants.' The article, describing the proximity to humans of a small herd of elephants near Victoria Falls, concludes:

> It is a thing of rare beauty nonetheless: Humans and dangerous animals at peace and in harmony with each other—proving once again that there is always something new out of Africa.

The immediate source of the saying is a passage in the *Natural History* of the Roman statesman and scholar Pliny the Elder. Explaining the number of African animals by hybridization (for example, lions breeding with leopards), Pliny explains that this is what gave rise to what he calls a common Greek saying that '**Africa always brings forth something new.**' The allusion is to a passage in Aristotle's *History of Animals* in which he notes that the most numerous forms of wild animals are to be found in Libya, and gives the saying '**Libya is always showing something new.**'

Ask not what your country can do for you

A famous question from the inaugural address of John Fitzgerald Kennedy in 1961. The passage from which it is taken runs:

> And so, my fellow Americans: ask not what your country can do for you—ask what you can do for your country. My fellow citizens of the world: ask not what America will do for you, but what together we can do for the freedom of man.

The question echoed, and slightly altered, the words of an earlier notable figure in American public life: Supreme Court Justice Oliver Wendell Holmes Jr. In a speech of 1884, Holmes had said: '**We pause to...recall what our country has done for each of us and to ask ourselves what we can do for our country in return.**'

Between Holmes in 1884 and Kennedy in 1961, a similar thought is found in the writings of the Lebanese-born writer and painter Kahlil Gibran, who wrote in *The New Frontier* (1931):

> Are you a politician who says to himself: 'I will use my country for my own benefit'?...Or are you a devoted patriot, who whispers in the ear of his inner self: 'I love to serve my country as a faithful servant.'

As Maine goes, so goes Vermont

In 1936, Franklin Roosevelt's campaign manager James A. Farley put out a statement to the press in which he correctly predicted that Roosevelt would carry all but two states, Maine and Vermont, in the presidential election of that year. Farley was reworking the saying '**As Maine goes, so goes the nation**' which, taking the results of the state of Maine as a sure indicator of success in a presidential election, had been an American political maxim since the mid nineteenth century.

Hugh Rawson and Margaret Miner, editors of the *Oxford Dictionary of American Quotations* (2004), suggest that the saying derived from the presidential and vice-presidential candidates of 1840, William Henry Harrison, known as the 'Hero of Tippecanoe', and John Tyler. Edward Kent had won election as Governor of Maine in the summer (until 1958 Maine voted in advance of the national election in November), and his victory was the precursor of national success for the Whigs. The Whig campaign song of 1840 ran:

> And have you heard the news from Maine,
> And what old Maine can do?
> She went hell-bent for Governor Kent,
> And Tippecanoe and Tyler too.'

Rawson and Miner add to their comments on Maine as an electoral indicator the note that it has in fact 'supported more presidential losers than any other state'.

It is also worth noting that the original form of the maxim is still firmly embedded in the public consciousness. An article in the *New York Times* in May 2003, entitled 'The Nation: Search Engine Society', had the subtitle '**As Google goes, so goes the nation**.'

Backing into the limelight

An assessment of the reaction to publicity of the soldier and writer T. E. Lawrence ('Lawrence of Arabia'), which has now become part of the wider language, as in Libby Brooks's 2003 account of an interview with the journalist John Simpson:

> He has...exhibited a talent for placing himself at the centre of the story that both confounds and enrages colleagues. He will concede to a habit of "backing into the limelight", but says that life is too short to worry about accusations of arrogance.

Oral tradition attributes to the composer and writer Lord Berners the comment on Lawrence '**He's always backing into the limelight**.' (Nigel Rees, in his 1997 *Cassell Companion to Quotations*, records it as being employed by Winston Churchill. Montague Brown, former secretary to Churchill, gave a speech to the International Churchill Society in 1985. In it, he quoted Churchill as saying of Lawrence, '**He had the art of backing uneasily into the limelight. He was a very remarkable character and very careful of that fact**.')

However, a much earlier use of a similar image is found in the diaries of the German diplomat Count Harry Kessler, relating a meeting with George Bernard Shaw in 1929. According to Shaw, Lawrence had complained that every move of his was followed by the Press. This elicited the Shavian response, 'You always hide just in the middle of the limelight.'

Backwards and in high heels

The comment that the actress and dancer Ginger Rogers did everything that her partner Fred Astaire did, but 'backwards and in high heels' and therefore with extra difficulty, is often attributed to Rogers herself. Rogers herself, however, denied it, although she recounted an anecdote which gave force to the expression. In her autobiography *My Story* (1991), she said that she generally practised in low heels, and changed to higher heels when filming. When choreographing 'Smoke Gets in Your Eyes', Fred Astaire forgot that she would be wearing high heels. As a result, trying to achieve 'a backwards three-step turn-jump up the stairs', she nearly lost her balance. She believed, though, that the actual line was the coinage of the cartoonist Bob Thaves.

Years after the near-fall she described, a friend sent her a cartoon by Bob Thaves, in his 'Frank and Ernest' series, from a Los Angeles newspaper. In the cartoon (which certainly popularized if it did not originate the saying), Frank and Ernest are shown gazing at a billboard announcing a Fred Astaire film festival. The caption reads: 'Sure he was great, but don't forget that Ginger Rogers did everything he did...backwards and in high heels.'

The phrase is often associated with the American Democratic politician Ann Richards, then Governor of Texas, who in her keynote address to the Democratic Convention of 1988 said:

> Twelve years ago Barbara Jordan, another Texas woman...made the keynote address to this convention, and two women in a hundred and sixty years is about par for the course. But if you give us a chance, we can

perform. After all, Ginger Rogers did everything that Fred Astaire did.
She just did it backwards and in high heels.

Bad money drives out good

A statement of the economic need to maintain the purity of the
currency, associated with the sixteenth-century founder of the
Royal Exchange, Sir Thomas Gresham, who was concerned with

'Bad money drives out good'

trying to restore the debased coinage of Elizabeth I's
reign. Although Gresham did not coin the saying,
he was familiar with the principle. In the nineteenth
century, the economist H. D. Macleod, recognizing
this, used the term 'Gresham's law' for the rule that
'where two media come into circulation at the same
time, the more valuable will tend to disappear.'

The ballot is stronger than the bullet

A succinct statement of the views of Abraham Lincoln, found
in a 1905 reconstruction of a speech given by him in 1856; the
sentence appears, 'Do not mistake that the ballot is stronger than
the bullet.' However, in the view of the editor of Lincoln's *Collected
Works*, Roy P. Basner, the reconstruction could not be accepted as
solid evidence of use. After that, the nearest expression of the view is
found in a speech of May 1858, in which Lincoln said, '**To give victory
to the right, not *bloody bullets*, but *peaceful ballots* only, are necessary.**'

There are other instances of Lincoln using these contrasting
images: he wrote in a letter of 1863 that 'There can be no successful
appeal from the ballot to the bullet.'

The battle of Waterloo was won on the playing fields of Eton

In his book *The Lion and the Unicorn* (1941), the novelist and essayist George Orwell wrote: '**Probably the battle of Waterloo *was* won on the playing-fields of Eton, but the opening battles of all subsequent wars have been lost there.**' This was a familiar reference: *Time* magazine in November 1939 carried an article headed 'Ploughing Fields of Eton'. It opened:

> As every British schoolboy has often been told, the battle of Waterloo was won on the playing fields of Eton. Last week Eton offered 15 acres of its famed Playing Field called Agar's Plough to the British Government for husbandry in the Grow-More-Food program. With respectful gratitude the Buckinghamshire Agricultural Committee touched its forelock and accepted.

In 1938, Noël Coward had included the line '**The playing-fields of Eton have made us frightfully brave**' in his song 'The Stately Homes of England', confident that the allusion would be immediately recognizable.

The original statement (in the form 'The battle of Waterloo was won in the playing fields of Eton') is attributed by oral tradition to the Duke of Wellington, but is probably apocryphal. The earliest version of it (recorded in 1856), said to have been uttered by the Duke when revisiting Eton, is '**It is here that the battle of Waterloo was won!**'

By 1881, it was evidently familiar enough to be used allusively, without direct reference to Wellington. Matthew Arnold, in an essay 'An Eton Boy', published in the *Fortnightly Review* of June of that year, wrote:

> The aged Barbarian [i.e. a member of the English upper classes] will, upon this, mumble to us his story how the battle of Waterloo was won in the playing-fields of Eton. Alas! disasters have been prepared in those

playing-fields as well as victories; disasters due to inadequate mental training—to want of application, knowledge, intelligence, lucidity.

It is interesting to note the degree to which his further comment foreshadowed Orwell.

Beam me up, Scotty

A column headed 'Scotty to be beamed up' in the *Sydney Morning Herald* of July 2005 announced the death of the actor James Doohan, who had played the engineer Montgomery Scott in the TV series *Star Trek*. The report included the information that it was planned to send his ashes into space. The phrase used, and its association, are both familiar; nearly three years before, a column in the *New York Times* for September 2002 had opened:

> Fans of futuristic 'Star Trek' and military technologies could only shiver in anticipation last week when scientists announced a breakthrough in the production of antimatter, the magical material that could supposedly whisk us at warp speed across the galaxy or blow us to smithereens in a cataclysmic explosion.

It was headed, 'Don't beam us up just yet.'

'Beam me up, Scotty', now used to indicate a desire to be removed from a dangerous or difficult situation, is supposedly the form in which Captain Kirk of the television series *Star Trek* (1966 onwards) habitually requested to be returned from a planet to the Starship *Enterprise*. In fact, the nearest equivalent found is, 'Beam us up, Mr. Scott', which occurs in Gene Roddenberry's 'Gamesters of Triskelion'.

A beginning, a muddle, and an end

John Gregory Dunne's *Monster: Living off the Big Screen*, published in 1997, gave a scriptwriter's view of the power of the 'monster': the effect on film-making of the anxiety to generate more and more money. One of the results of this was to turn out scripts intended only as vehicles for stars. Larry Gelbart, reviewing the book in the *New York Times* of March 1997, wrote: 'Such scripts tend to be filled with any number of plot holes…Increasingly, to court and to please the stars, the monster is turning out pictures that have a beginning, a muddle and an end.'

The phrase had been used earlier for the 'classic formula' for a novel, as outlined by the poet Philip Larkin in 1978. Larkin was reworking a line from a much earlier original, a passage from Aristotle's *Poetics*:

> A whole is that which has a beginning, a middle, and an end. A beginning is that which does not itself follow anything by causal necessity, but after which something naturally is or comes to be. An end, on the contrary, is that which itself naturally follows some other thing, either by necessity, or as a rule, but has nothing following it. A middle is that which follows something as some other thing follows it. A well-constructed plot, therefore, must neither begin nor end haphazard, but conform to these principles.

The best-laid plans of mice and men

An alteration of the original words of Robert Burns, which has established itself in the language as a way to express resignation at careful forethought failing to achieve success. The original lines, in Burns's poem 'To a Mouse' (1786), were:

> The best laid schemes o' mice an' men
> Gang aft agley.

Books do furnish a room

In 1971, Anthony Powell published a novel in his 'Dance to the Music of Time' sequence entitled *Books do Furnish a Room*. It seems probable that this reflects a comment by the nineteenth-century clergyman and wit Sydney Smith, 'No furniture so charming as books'.

The British are coming!

In 1981, receiving an Oscar for the screenplay of the film *Chariots of Fire*, the British actor and screenwriter Colin Welland announced to the crowd that 'The British are coming!'

The words are famously said to be the cry of warning raised by the American patriot Paul Revere on the night of 18 April 1775. Revere had been instructed to ride to Lexington to warn his fellow revolutionaries, John Hancock and Samuel Adams, that troops were marching west from Boston; he also warned several farms on the route to Lexington. However, it has been pointed out that neither Revere nor William Hawes (a second rider sent by a separate route) would have cried 'The British are coming!', since at that time most of their hearers would still have regarded themselves as British. It is likely that the warning was something similar to 'The Regulars are coming out!'

'The British are coming!'

The ride (as by Paul Revere alone) was made famous by Henry Wadsworth Longfellow's poem 'Paul Revere's Ride' (from *Tales of a Wayside Inn* 'The Landlord's Tale', 1863). Longfellow does not use the phrase 'the British are coming', but he does use the anachronistic 'British' in 'If the British march', words attributed to Revere.

The budget should be balanced. . .

The *Congressional Record* of 25 April 1968 attributes to the Roman orator and statesman Marcus Tullius Cicero (106–43 BC) a long passage of advice on economic and fiscal responsibility:

> The budget should be balanced, the treasury should be refilled, public debt should be reduced, the arrogance of officialdom should be tempered and controlled, assistance to foreign lands should be curtailed lest Rome should become bankrupt, the mobs should be forced to work and not depend on government for subsistence.

15 Build a better mousetrap, and they will beat a path to your door

Since 1968, this has been widely quoted, but it has never been traced in Cicero's works.

Build a better mousetrap, and they will beat a path to your door

The 'better mousetrap' is now part of our vocabulary. In 2001, Adam Hart-Davis's *What the Victorians Did for Us* television progamme showed a 'mighty multiple mousetrap', which could catch twenty-eight mice in a night. The critic Nancy Banks-Smith, reviewing the programme, commented 'This must have been the legendary better mousetrap, which makes the world beat a path to your door.'

The popular form of the advice is attributed to the American philosopher and poet Ralph Waldo Emerson. In its original form, it read:

> If a man write a better book, preach a better sermon, or make a better mouse-trap than his neighbour, tho' he build his house in the woods, the world will make a beaten path to his door.

It was attributed to Emerson in 1889 by Sarah Yule, in *Borrowings*, an anthology compiled by the 'Ladies of the First Unitarian Church of Oakland, California'. She subsequently (in 1912) stated that she copied it from a lecture delivered by Emerson in 1871. Emerson's own writings contain only a considerably longer version, in his journal for February 1855:

> I trust a good deal to common fame, as we all must. If a man has good corn, or wood, or boards, or pigs, to sell, or can make better chairs or knives, crucibles or church organs, than anybody else, you will find a broad hard-beaten road to his house.

In the tenth edition of *The Home Book of Quotations* (1967), Burton Stevenson noted that the writer Elbert Hubbard, who included the saying in his 1911 compilation *A Thousand and One Epigrams*, later claimed that it was his own coinage (he had also previously used it, in a slightly different form, in 1895). He said that 'he saved his modesty and at the same time gave his epigram specific gravity, by attributing it to one Ralph Waldo Emerson'. However, as Stevenson pointed out, Sarah Yule's 1889 publication predated Stevenson's earliest usage. He concluded that 'It is certain that Hubbard did not originate the quotation.'

The capitalists will sell us the rope with which to hang them

A prediction attributed to Lenin, but not found in any of his works. A manuscript note said to be by him, giving the same idea, but in much longer form, was published in 'Reminiscences of Lenin' in the *New Review* of September 1961:

> They [capitalists] will furnish credits which will serve us for the support of the Communist Party in their countries and, by supplying us materials and technical equipment which we lack, will restore our military industry necessary for our future attacks against our suppliers. To put it in other words, they will work on the preparation of their own suicide.

A chicken in every pot

During the US presidential campaign of 1928, the eventual victor, the Republican Herbert Hoover, said that 'The slogan of progress is changing from the full dinner pail to the full garage.' This is often paraphrased as 'a car in every garage and a chicken in every pot'—or even, as an article in the *Guardian* of June 2004 discussing John Kerry's US presidential campaign ironically suggested: 'I think the pot-of-gold retirement strategy is a way to work. Forget a chicken in every pot. It's time for a Winnebago in every driveway.'

The wording of the paraphrase echoes the aspiration of a much earlier head of state, Henri of Navarre, who from 1589 was King of France: 'I want there to be no peasant in my kingdom so poor that he is unable to have a chicken in his pot every Sunday.'

A child is not a vase to be filled, but a fire to be lit

A 2006 website for a New York summer camp for children included the words 'Operating under the philosophy that "a child is not a vase to be filled, but a fire to be lit."'

The words are now widely attributed to the sixteenth-century French humanist and satirist François Rabelais. However, the thought at least appears to be traceable back to a much earlier original, the Greek philosopher Plutarch of the first century AD. In his *Moralia*, Plutarch wrote: 'For the mind does not require filling like a bottle, but rather, like wood, it only requires kindling to create in it an impulse to think independently and an ardent desire for the truth.' Presumably this could be seen as one more example of the Renaissance drawing on the resources of the classical world.

City of dreaming spires

In *The Glittering Prizes* (1976), the writer Frederic Raphael coined for Cambridge the name 'City of perspiring dreams'. It was a neat allusion to a more established name for Oxford, as in Tom Stoppard's 1997 play *The Invention of Love*. The character representing A. E. Housman in old age says: 'That was more than fifty years ago, when Oxford was still the sweet city of dreaming spires.'

The name derives, with a small alteration, from a line in Matthew Arnold's 1866 poem 'Thyrsis': 'And that sweet City with her dreaming spires.'

A cold coming we had of it

T. S. Eliot's poem 'Journey of the Magi' (1927) opens with the evocative lines

A cold coming we had of it,
Just the worst time of the year.

Eliot was borrowing this effective setting from a much earlier writer, the seventeenth-century English sermon-writer and bishop Lancelot Andrewes. In his sermon 'On the Nativity' (1616) Andrewes had written on the same topic:

> It was no summer progress. A cold coming they had of it, at this time of the year; just, the worst time of the year, to take a journey, and specially a long journey, in. The ways deep, the weather sharp, the days short, the sun farthest off *in solstitio brumali*, the very dead of Winter.

Come with me to the Casbah

An invitation supposedly issued by the French actor Claude Boyer as the thief 'Pepe le Moko' to Hedy Lamarr's wealthy tourist Gaby, in the 1938 film *Algiers*. In fact, the line does not occur in the film. Pepe's situation is that he is trapped in the Casbah. If he leaves its shelter, he will be arrested by the police. (At one stage, Gaby asks wistfully, '**Can't you ever get away from the Casbah?**') However (as the *American National Biography* points out), Boyer became 'eternally identified' with the line 'come wiz me to the Casbah.' Boyer, who wanted to be seen as a serious actor, felt himself dogged by the assumption that he should appear in romantic roles. He is quoted as having said that '**I would say that one line, more than anything else, has hampered my career.**'

'Come with me to the Casbah'

Comment is free, but facts are on expenses

In Tom Stoppard's play *Night and Day* (1978), one of the characters, the foreign correspondent Dick Wagner, is exchanging quotations from the world of journalism with President Mageeba. The President, noting of one quotation that 'we had all that at the LSE' adds: '**And C. P. Scott of the *Manchester Guardian*, of course—"comment is free, but facts are sacred."**' Wagner responds: '**Yes, and "comment is free but facts are on expenses."**'

C. P. Scott was Editor (and proprietor) of the *Manchester Guardian*. In 1921, to celebrate the centenary of the paper and his fiftieth anniversary as editor, he wrote an essay entitled 'A Hundred Years', which was published in the *Guardian* on the fifth of May 1921. In one passage, he set out what he saw as the role of a newspaper:

> Its primary office is the gathering of news. At the peril of its soul it must see that the supply is not tainted. Neither in what it gives, nor in what it does not give, nor in the mode of presentation must the unclouded face of truth suffer wrong. Comment is free, but facts are sacred. 'Propaganda', so called, by this means is hateful. The voice of opponents no less than that of friends has a right to be heard. Comment also is justly subject to a self-imposed restraint. It is well to be frank; it is even better to be fair.

Consistency is the hobgoblin of little minds

Now often used ironically to criticize a failure to be consistent. However, the original passage from which this comes (the essay 1841 'Self-Reliance' by Ralph Waldo Emerson) inserted a qualifying 'foolish' before 'consistency'. The passage runs:

> A foolish consistency is the hobgoblin of little minds, adored by little statesmen and philosophers and divines. With consistency a great soul has simply nothing to do.

It is possible to take this as a protest against over-rigidity, rather than the assertion that consistency is in itself something that only a 'little mind' would consider important.

A contemptible little army

Shortly after the outbreak of the First World War, the British Expeditionary Force Routine Orders of 24 September 1914 included what was allegedly a copy of Orders issued to his forces by Kaiser Wilhelm II. The text ran as follows:

> The following is a copy of Orders issued by the German Emperor on August 19th: 'It is my Royal and Imperial command that you concentrate your energies for the immediate present upon one single purpose, and

that is that you address all your skill and all the valour of my soldiers to exterminate first, the treacherous English, walk over General French's contemptible little army...

Headquarters, Aix la Chapelle, August 19th.'

The Routine Orders went on to say that:

The results of the order were the operations commencing with Mons, and the advance of the seemingly overwhelming masses against us. The answer of the British Army on the subject of extermination has already been given.

The politician and peace campaigner Arthur Ponsonby devoted a chapter of *Falsehood in Wartime*, his 1928 account of the use of propaganda, to 'the contemptible little army'. Ponsonby opened his account by noting that the message attributed to the Kaiser 'very naturally created a passionate feeling of resentment throughout the country'. He quoted a *Times* leader of 1 October 1914 as saying that '**In spite of the ferocious order of the Kaiser... "French's contemptible little army" is not yet exterminated.**' He went on to describe a spate of further references and allusions, including a number of cartoons, which showed that the supposed order was still remembered and resented.

Ponsonby went on to confirm that careful enquiries made after the war had failed to identify the order in the German archives. The ex-Kaiser denied that he had given any such order, and it was pointed out that the German Headquarters were never based at Aix la Chapelle. General Frederick Maurice had had the files of German newspapers searched without success, and said in an article in the *Daily News* of November 1925 that the Army had had a system of using routine orders to promulgate statements that would inspire and encourage the troops. 'Most of these took the form of casting ridicule on the German Army...These efforts were seen to be absurd by the men in the trenches, and were soon dropped.'

Subsequently, 'the Old Contemptibles' became a popular name

given to the British army of regulars and special reserve sent to France in the autumn of 1914.

It is interesting to note a much earlier use of the adjective in a military context. Oliver Cromwell, in a speech to Parliament in April 1657 said: 'Your poor army, those poor contemptible men, came up hither.'

Corporations have neither bodies to be punished nor souls to be damned

A proverbial statement of the position of a large organization in its exemption from the sanctions to which an individual is liable, which derives from formulations of earlier centuries. Lord Thurlow, an eighteenth-century Lord Chancellor, is quoted in John Poynder's *Literary Extracts* of 1844 as saying that 'Corporations have neither bodies to be punished, not souls to be condemned, they therefore do as they like.' (Thurlow has also been quoted less formally as saying, 'Did you ever expect a corporation to have a conscience, when it has no soul to be damned, and no body to be kicked?')

A similar thought is found in the writings of the seventeenth-century English jurist, Edward Coke: 'They [corporations] cannot commit treason, nor be outlawed, nor excommunicate, for they have no souls.'

A covenant with death, and an agreement with hell

In January 1843 the Massachusetts Anti-Slavery Society adopted a resolution formulated by the abolitionist campaigner William Lloyd Garrison that 'The compact which exists between the North and the South is "a covenant with death and an agreement with hell".' (As the *American National Biography* points out, in the previous year Garrison had charged that the United States Constitution was '"a covenant with death—an agreement with hell" that had been designed by the Founding Fathers to secure the perpetuity of slavery'.)

The condemnatory phrases of the resolution had direct biblical echoes, in the Authorized Version's translation of the Old Testament book of Isaiah: 'We have made a covenant with death, and with hell are we at agreement.' (A few verses later, comes the warning 'Your covenant with death shall be disannulled, and your agreement with hell shall not stand.')

Crisis? What Crisis?

In January 1979, the Labour Government was struggling with the effects of the widespread strikes generated by the 'winter of discontent'. The Prime Minister, James Callaghan, returned to London from a meeting of Commonwealth leaders held in Guadeloupe. Interviewed at Heathrow, he was asked to comment on the domestic situation. His response was a measured, 'I don't think other people in the world would share the view there is mounting chaos.' The following day, the *Sun* newspaper reported the interview under the headline, 'Crisis? What Crisis?'

Although it was generally recognized that these were not Callaghan's words, they nevertheless carried a damaging implication that the Prime Minister was out of touch with a situation in which the general public was struggling.

Culture is the best which has been thought and said

Often attributed in this form to the poet and essayist Matthew Arnold. The novelist Martin Amis, discussing the writing of fiction after the horrors of 11 September 2001 ('nine-eleven') in the *Guardian* of June 2002, considered the question of belief, and his own position as an agnostic. He identified the 'assertion of mortal pride' as a necessary 'humanistic counterweight' to belief. Amis went on:

A contemporary manifestation of this need can be seen in our intensified reverence for the planet (James Lovelock's Gaia and other benign animisms). A strategy with a rather longer history centres on an intensified reverence for art—or, in Matthew Arnold's formula, for 'the best which has been thought and said'.

What Arnold actually said was that culture was **'a pursuit of our total perfection by means of getting to know, on all the matters which most concern us, the best which has been thought and said in the world'**. The full passage (from the preface to Arnold's 1869 *Culture and Anarchy*) runs:

> The whole scope of the essay is to recommend culture as the great help out of our present difficulties; culture being a pursuit of our total perfection by means of getting to know, on all the matters which most concern us, the best which has been thought and said in the world, and, through this knowledge, turning a stream of fresh and free thought upon our stock notions and habits, which we now follow staunchly but mechanically, vainly imagining that there is a virtue in following them staunchly which makes up for the mischief of following them mechanically.

Dark forces at work

In November 2002, the case against the former royal butler Paul Burrell for taking property belonging to his late employer, Diana, Princess of Wales, collapsed dramatically when the Queen recalled a conversation with him in the aftermath of the Princess's death. While the point of this was that he had told the Queen that he was taking charge of some property for safekeeping, the conversation was said by Burrell to have included a warning about his personal safety, since **'There are powers at work in this country about which we have no knowledge.'**

'Dark forces at work'

The words were reported in an interview in the *Daily Mirror*, and subsequently appeared in other papers: the *Times* headed its account, 'The Queen "warned butler to beware of dark forces at work."'

Subsequent comment suggested considerable scepticism as to the Queen's use of this kind of language (an account in one website on conspiracy theory was headed, 'Ma'am and the Dark Forces'). More recently, in his book *Truth* (2005), the philosopher Simon Blackburn has given it as his view that she is unlikely to have said any such thing, while elaborating on the key phrase as a figure of speech: 'The dark forces of language, culture, power, gender, class, economic status, ideology and desire are always assailing us, but their work remains dangerously hidden in our blind spots.'

Dark night of the soul

A report in the *Guardian* of December 1970 commented that, 'Governor Nelson Rockefeller...has emerged from the dark night of the soul that afflicts all politicians pondering the supreme sacrifice.'

The phrase 'dark night of the soul' was notably used in the 20th century by the American writer F. Scott Fitzgerald. In 'Handle with Care', published in 1936, he wrote:

> The standard cure for one who is sunk is to consider those in actual destitution or physical suffering...But at three o'clock in the morning, a forgotten package has the same tragic importance as a death sentence, and the cure doesn't work—and in a real dark night of the soul it is always three o'clock in the morning.

The sixteenth-century Spanish mystic and poet St John of the Cross was the author of a poem '*Noche oscura* [Dark night]', which appeared as part of *The Ascent of Mount Carmel*. Three centuries later, in a translation of the complete works of St John of the Cross, the translator, David Lewis, gave 'Faith, the dark night of the soul' as a chapter heading for the poem.

The decent obscurity of a learned language

A phrase which has now entered the language to suggest a degree (and method) of censorship. A review in the *New York Review of Books* for November 1988 included an anecdote about the Latin scholar and poet A. E. Housman, who in 1931 had offered to the leading British classical journal a set of notes on a number of obscene Latin poems. 'Although presented in what Gibbon calls "the decent obscurity of a learned language", to wit Latin, his contribution was rejected.' (It was apparently subsequently published in Germany.)

Supposedly coined by Edward Gibbon, the phrase actually comes from a parody in the *Anti-Jacobin* (1797–8), a journal founded by the Tory statesman George Canning and his friends to combat (and satirize) radical views. What Gibbon had actually said of his writings (in *Memoirs of My Life*, 1796) was: 'My English text is chaste, and all licentious passages are left in the obscurity of a learned language.'

It is worth noting that in *The Decline and Fall of the Roman Empire*, Gibbon did actually use the phrase 'decent obscurity'. He points out in a footnote that the French historian Tillemont, writing of St Cyril, has 'thrown his virtues into the text, and his faults in to the notes, in decent obscurity, at the end of the volume'.

A democracy, if you can keep it

In January 2006, a search for the string 'Democracy, if you can keep it' returned nearly 500 hits on Google. In the majority of cases, the words were attributed to the American statesman, and signatory to the Declaration of Independence, Benjamin Franklin, asked what kind of state the new American nation would be.

The original form of Franklin's rejoinder is recorded in the diary of James McHenry (1753–1816), who in 1778 was appointed as secretary to George Washington. McHenry recorded in his diary that on one occasion, a Mrs Powel of Philadelphia asked Franklin: 'Well

Doctor what have we got a republic or a monarchy?' Franklin's reply, as noted by McHenry, was, '**A republic if you can keep it.**'

Deputy sheriff in the region

In October 2003, George W. Bush was asked about the tag of 'deputy sheriff', as applied to Australia's role in the Asia Pacific region in relation to the United States. He replied: '**We don't see it as deputy sheriff. We see it as a sheriff, equal partners, friends and allies.**' A few days later, John Howard, Prime Minister of Australia, gave an interview in which he said: '**Can I make it very clear. I don't see this country as being a sheriff, a deputy sheriff, as having any kind of enforcement role in our region.**'

Both answers looked back to a widely reported interview of September 1999. The journalist Fred Brenchley, interviewing John Howard, indicated how he thought the Prime Minister saw Australia's role in relation to America (as deputy). John Howard added 'in the region'. It was subsequently reported (with widespread resentment, both at home and abroad) that the Prime Minister himself had used the term 'deputy sheriff'. While it now seems to be generally accepted that he did not use the words, it also seems clear that the expression, and the resentment caused by the reports, will be remembered.

Dissent is the highest form of patriotism

An assertion frequently attributed to Thomas Jefferson, but which in fact seems to be a modern coinage, although one without clear attribution. The American historian Howard Zinn is recorded as saying, in July 2002:

> While some people think that dissent is unpatriotic, I would argue that dissent is the highest form of patriotism. In fact, if patriotism means being true to the principles for which your country is supposed to stand, then certainly the right to dissent is one of those principles.

An earlier use than Zinn's is found (and a still earlier possibility indicated) in the Library of Congress's *Information Bulletin* for May 2002. In 'Responding to September 11', an account of a symposium on terrorism held at the Library, Janice Hyde noted that:

> Roger Wilkins, a professor of history at George Mason University, related an incident during the time of the Vietnam War in which he argued that 'dissent is the highest form of patriotism and the highest form of loyalty.'

Whatever its twentieth-century origins, it seems unlikely to be a genuine quotation from Jefferson, who wrote in a letter of May 1797:

> Political dissension is doubtless a less evil than the lethargy of despotism, but still it is a great evil, and it would be as worthy the efforts of the patriot as of the philosopher, to exclude its influence, if possible, from social life.

Don't unchain the tiger

Supposedly an appeal from a letter written by Benjamin Franklin to the freethinking radical Tom Paine, in an attempt to dissuade Paine from publishing *The Age of Reason* (1794). The relevant passage of this letter, published in the *Collected Works of Benjamin Franklin* (1840), edited by Jared Sparks, read: 'I would advise you, therefore, not to attempt unchaining the tiger, but to burn this piece before it is seen by any other person.'

'Don't unchain the tiger'

The letter is undated, and no recipient is named. Moreover (as Paul F. Boller, Jr. and John George point out in *They Never Said It*, 1989), Franklin died in 1790, before Paine started work on *The Age of Reason*.

It is of interest that 'Don't unchain the tiger' was used in nineteenth-century America in other contexts as a warning against terrible consequences. It appears in an anti-Southern broadsheet printed in New York in July 1863, with authorship attributed to 'A Democratic Workingman'. The first paragraph reads:

> When the Traitors of South Carolina met in convention in Charleston,
> and passed their ordinance to abolish the American Union, to crush out
> the democratic principles of free government in America, and when they
> afterwards fired upon Fort Sumter, and I knew that secession meant a
> terrible war, I said to myself and to them—*Don't unchain the Tiger!*

The broadsheet, having warned dramatically against the dangers of
those trying to 'get the Workingmen aroused to deeds of crime and
violence', concludes:

> The patriotric Workingmen of the North cannot afford to spend time
> killing each other. Be wise, and above all things, DON'T UNCHAIN THE TIGER!

Do what thou wilt shall be the whole of the law

A principle formulated by the English diabolist Aleister Crowley,
in his *Book of the Law* (1909), although its origins are remote in
time and thought from Crowley.

In the sixteenth century, the French humanist and satirist
François Rabelais offered (in *Gargantua*, 1534) a motto in which
prospective action was similarly free from moral control: '*Fay ce
que vouldras* [Do what you like].' Originally, however, the Roman
Christian theologian St Augustine of Hippo, writing in the early
fifth century, had indicated a model in which the personal will
would be guided by right feeling, with the principle '*Dilige et quod vis
fac* [Love and do what you will].'

Dreams are the royal road to the unconscious

A popular summary of the views of the Austrian psychiatrist
Sigmund Freud, which has now become part of our vocabulary.
(The critic John Sutherland, writing in 2001 on the vocabulary of
President Bush, commented, '**As Sigmund Freud reminds us, the
lapsus linguae is, like the dream, a royal road to the unconscious.**')
However, what Freud actually wrote, in *The Interpretation of Dreams*

(2nd edition, 1909), was: 'The interpretation of dreams is the royal road to a knowledge of the unconscious activities of the mind.'

The dwarf sees farther than the giant

In 1999 Melvyn Bragg published *On Giant's Shoulders*, an account of great scientists from Archimedes to the discoverers of DNA. In choosing the title, he was using a long-established image to reach back through the centuries.

The English poet and philosopher Samuel Taylor Coleridge wrote in *The Friend* (1818) that 'The dwarf sees farther than the giant, when he has the giant's shoulder to mount on.' In 1676 the mathematician and physicist Isaac Newton had written to his fellow scientist Robert Hooke that 'If I have seen further it is by standing on the shoulders of giants.' Both references echo a much earlier thinker; in the 12th century, the French philosopher Bernard of Chartres had written:

> We are like dwarfs on the shoulders of giants, so that we can see more than they, and things at a greater distance, not by virtue of any sharpness of sight on our part, or any physical distinction, but because we are carried high and raised up by their giant size.

Economical with the truth

In 1986 the British civil servant and former Cabinet Secretary, Sir Robert Armstrong, was giving evidence to the 'Spycatcher' case in the Supreme Court of New South Wales. (The British Government was attempting to prevent publication of the memoirs of the former MI5 agent Peter Wright.) Referring to a letter, Sir Robert said, 'It contains a misleading impression, not a lie. It was being economical with the truth.'

The key phrase quickly became notorious. It was subsequently (in the Matrix Churchill trial) reworked by the Conservative politician and former junior Minister Alan Clark, as 'Our old friend... economical with the actualité'.

In the nineteenth century, Mark Twain pointed out, in *Following the Equator* (1897), that 'Truth is the most valuable thing we have. Let us economize it.' There is, however, an even earlier related usage, from the political world, to be found in the writings of the Whig politician Edmund Burke. In *Two Letters on the Proposals for Peace with the Regicide Directory* (1796) he said: 'Falsehood and delusion are allowed in no case whatsoever: But, as in the exercise of all the virtues, there is an economy of truth.'

Elementary, my dear Watson

This remark, as attributed to the detective Sherlock Holmes, is taken as typifying the relationship between him and his faithful friend and amanuensis, Dr Watson. However, it is not found in this form in any of Conan Doyle's stories, and first appears in P. G. Wodehouse's *Psmith, Journalist* (1915). Psmith, having said that 'this is one of those moments when it is necessary for me to unlimber my Sherlock Holmes system', gives his explanation of what has happened to a slower companion. When this is received with approbation, Psmith murmurs 'Elementary, my dear Watson, elementary.'

The nearest thing to it in Conan Doyle's own work is an exchange recorded by Watson in *The Memoirs of Sherlock Holmes* (1894) 'The Crooked Man': '"Excellent," I cried. "Elementary," said he.'

An empty taxi drew up outside 10 Downing Street and Attlee got out

A quip which, in the aftermath of the Labour landslide of 1945, was attributed to Winston Churchill.

Churchill is on record with a number of cutting comments about the Labour leader, of which 'a sheep in sheep's clothing' is only one. However, when this remark was repeated to him by his former principal private secretary, the civil servant and diplomat

John Colville, Churchill immediately rejected the comment on his
successor as Prime Minister.

> Mr Attlee is an honourable and gallant gentleman, and a faithful
> colleague who served his country well at the time of her greatest need. I
> should be obliged if you would make it clear whenever an occasion arises
> that I would never make such a remark about him, and that I strongly
> disapprove of anybody who does.

Engineers of the soul

In a speech at Amherst College, Massachusetts, 26 October 1963,
President John F. Kennedy said, '**In free society,
Art is not a weapon...Artists are not engineers
of the soul**.' His allusion was to a Soviet usage
of three decades before. The Russian writer and
revolutionary Maxim Gorky had said in a speech to
the Writers' Congress of 1934 that '**The proletarian
state must bring up thousands of "mechanics of culture", "engineers
of the soul"**.' However, the coinage of this term appears to rest with
Joseph Stalin. In a speech to writers at Gorky's house, 26 October
1932, he said:

'Engineers of the soul'

> There are various forms of production: artillery, automobiles, lorries. You
> also produce 'commodities', 'works', 'products'. Such things are highly
> necessary. Engineering things. For people's souls. 'Products' are highly
> necessary too. 'Products' are very important for people's souls. You are
> engineers of human souls.

England and America are two countries divided by a common language

A view widely attributed (in this and other forms) to the dramatist
and critic George Bernard Shaw, but which has not been traced
in Shaw's published writings. A similar thought, however, can be
found in Oscar Wilde's *The Canterville Ghost* (1887), in the description

of the American Mrs Otis, whose wealthy husband has bought
Canterville Chase from its impoverished owner, Lord Canterville:

> She had a magnificent constitution, and a really wonderful amount
> of animal spirits. Indeed, in many respects she was quite English, and
> was an excellent example of the fact that we have really everything in
> common with America nowadays except, of course, language.

The English are a nation of shopkeepers

An assessment now generally attributed to Napoleon, and
certainly the comment was attributed to the ex-Emperor by his
personal surgeon, Barry O'Meara, who was part of his household
on St Helena. However, the association of English political power
with commerce was already established, as is shown by this passage
from *The Wealth of Nations* (1776) by the Scottish philosopher and
economist Adam Smith:

> To found a great empire for the sole purpose of raising up a people
> of customers, may at first sight appear a project fit only for a nation
> of shopkeepers. It is, however, a project altogether unfit for a nation
> of shopkeepers; but extremely fit for a nation whose government is
> influenced by shopkeepers.

The even tenor of one's way

An obituary of the former Premier of Canada, the Liberal
statesman Pierre Trudeau, appeared in the Toronto *Globe and
Mail* of September 2000. At one point, the obituary considered
the impact of the separatist issue on Canadian politics, in relation
to Trudeau and his opponent René Lévesque, the founder of the
Parti Québecois. It reflected that, 'for all the friction introduced
to "the even tenor of our ways", our national drama brought on a
marvellous human convergence, Lévesque and Trudeau'.

The phrase 'the even tenor of one's way' to express the idea of
a settled and comfortable way of life is an established one. The
Mechanic's Press (Utica, New York) for December 1829 carried the

comment, 'His Rip Van Winkleish habits asked no more than to pursue "the even tenor of their way".' Interestingly, however, it appears to represent a small change from the wording of the original from which it is drawn, which also reflects a shift in sense. The lines from Gray's *Elegy Writtten in a Country Churchyard* (1751) evoke not just a settled life which is not disturbed, but also a solitary one which by implication does not disturb or catch the attention of others:

> Along the cool sequestered vale of life
> They kept the noiseless tenor of their way.

The novelist Tom Sharpe, in his 1973 satirical comic novel *Indecent Exposure*, set in apartheid South Africa, reworked the changed phrase further with the line, 'The South African police would leave no stone unturned to see that nothing disturbed the even terror of their lives.'

Events, dear boy. Events

Popular version of what is said to have been Harold Macmillan's response on being asked what was his biggest problem as Prime Minister. The words have become part of the political lexicon to describe the limitations of the most careful planning and foresight. In one recent example, the journalist William Keegan, in a *Guardian* column of October 2005, referred to 'the economic storms caused by Harold Macmillan's notorious "events, dear boy, events"'. There is however no verifiable source for the comment in this form: the nearest to it is 'The opposition of events'. (David Dilks, in a lecture on 'The Office of the Prime Minister in Twentieth-Century Britain', given in 1992, commented that 'A prime minister needs luck, to confront what Mr Macmillan so finely called "the opposition of events".' A note in Peter Hennessy's *The Hidden Wiring* (1995) adds that Professor Dilks, who had helped Macmillan with his memoirs from time to time, said that this was a phrase 'of which he was rather fond'.)

Nevertheless, the words 'Events, dear boy. Events' are taken as typifying Macmillan's public persona, and his deliberately cultivated old-world manner (Colin Matthew, in his *Oxford Dictionary of National Biography*, referred to 'the character of the "gent" which Macmillan so sedulously exploited').

Facts are stupid things

Often represented as a misquotation by Ronald Reagan of the words of John Adams (lawyer and later second President of the United States), defending soldiers in the 'Boston Massacre' trials. In March 1770, soldiers deployed in Boston to maintain order fired into a crowd, and several people were killed. In the subsequent trials, John Adams appeared for the defence. In the course of his speech, he uttered the words:

'Facts are stupid things'

> Facts are stubborn things; and whatever may be our wishes, our inclinations, or the dictates of our passions, they cannot alter the states of facts and evidence.

In his address to the 1988 Republican National Convention, Ronald Reagan introduced a section of his speech with the words:

> Before we came to Washington, Americans had just suffered the two worst back-to-back years of inflation in 60 years. Those are the facts, and as John Adams said, 'Facts are stubborn things.'

This paragraph, and the following four paragraphs, finished with Adams's words. However, at the end of the third paragraph, Reagan made a verbal slip, which he immediately corrected. A transcript of the speech reads, '**Facts are stupid things—stubborn things, I should say. [Laughter]**.' However, despite its origin as a slip of the tongue, 'Facts are stupid things' has taken on a life of its own in the world of quotations.

Failure is not an option

In the screenplay of the 1995 film *Apollo 13*, these words are spoken by, and encapsulate the philosophy of, the American former NASA flight director Gene Kranz. In 1970, Kranz was the lead flight director for the Apollo 13 mission. An explosion in the service module was signalled to Mission Control by the words of the astronaut James Lovell: '**Houston, we've had a problem.**' It meant that Kranz's team in the Control Center at Houston was responsible for bringing the astronauts safely back to earth in a damaged spacecraft. In the film Kranz (played by Ed Harris) says, '**We've never lost an American in space, we're sure as hell not going to lose one on my watch! Failure is not an option.**'

Kranz used 'Failure is not an option' as the title of his autobiography, published in 2000 (it includes his view that 'Failure does not exist in the lexicon of a flight controller.'). But while his account of what he said to his team does not include the words, they clearly summarize the spirit of the concluding passage of his briefing:

> When you leave this room, you must leave believing that *this crew is coming home*. I don't give a damn about the odds and I don't give a damn that we've never done anything like this before. Flight control will *never* lose an American in space. You've got to believe, your people have got to believe, that this crew is coming home. Now let's get going!

Fate knocking at the door

Words attributed to Beethoven as summarizing the initial motif of the Fifth Symphony. Many years after the composer's death, his secretary Anton Schindler wrote:

> The composer himself provided the key to these depths when one day, in his author's presence, he pointed to the beginning of the first movement and expressed in these words the fundamental idea of his work: 'Thus Fate knocks at the door!'

Unfortunately, Schindler is not regarded as a reliable witness: it has been pointed out that his biography of Beethoven contained many inaccuracies, and he has also been demonstrated to have included forgeries in the Beethoven conversation-books.

A feather on the breath of God

In the early 1980s, *A Feather on the Breath of God* was the title of a best-selling recording of the hymns and sequences of the twelfth-century German abbess, composer, and mystic Hildegard of Bingen. The words 'I am a feather on the breath of God' are often quoted as a personal statement by Hildegard. They appear to summarize a much longer passage, from a letter to Odo of Soissons, written in 1148:

> 'Listen now! A king sat on his throne, high pillars before him splendidly adorned and set on pediments of ivory....Then the king chose to lift a small feather from the ground, and he commanded it to fly just as the king himself wished. But a feather does not fly of its own accord, it is borne up by the air. So too I am not imbued with human doctrine or strong powers...Rather, I depend entirely on God's help.

Fellow immigrants

A form of address supposedly used in 1938 by President Franklin D. Roosevelt when addressing the Daughters of the American Revolution

Roosevelt in fact did not address the assembled ladies as 'My fellow immigrants'. (William Safire, in a 2001 column in the *New York Times* on possible openings to a presidential speech, notes that while 'My friends' became Roosevelt's 'signature opening', 'My fellow immigrants' to the DAR is legend.) However, FDR did urge his audience to: '**Remember, remember always that all of us, and you and I especially, are descended from immigrants and revolutionists.**'

Few die and none resign

An assessment of the human tendency to hold on to office, which for many years has been attributed in this form to Thomas Jefferson. Edward Deering Mansfield, in an 1868 life of Ulysses S. Grant, gave it as follows:

> Jefferson, with whom the old Democratic Party came into power, made a few removals, and was censured for it by his opponents. It was on that occasion that he made the celebrated reply, 'Few die and none resign.'

It is clearly what Jefferson thought, but his expression was slightly more measured. Considering the question, he asked in a letter of 1801, **'If a due participation of office is a matter of right, how are vacancies to be obtained? Those by death are few; by resignation none.'**

Fiery the angels fell

In *Blade Runner*, Ridley Scott's 1982 science fiction film set in 2020, 'replicants' (robots created to perform menial tasks for Earth's population in outer space) are forbidden to visit Earth. The penalty for being found there is destruction. At the opening of the film, four rebel replicants have nevertheless reached earth, and are concealing themselves in Los Angeles. Their leader, Roy Batty, entering the laboratory of a scientist who makes eyes for replicants, announces himself with the words:

> Fiery the angels fell, deep thunder rolled
> Around their shores: indignant burning with the fires of Orc.

Batty is misquoting William Blake's *America a Prophecy* (1793): the first line should be 'Fiery the angels rose, & as they rose deep thunder roll'd.'

First catch your hare

A proverbial warning against overconfidence, often thought to have originated in a recipe for hare soup in Mrs Glasse's *The Art of Cookery Made Plain and Easy* (1747) or Mrs Beeton's *Book of Household Management* (1851). It does not appear in either book, although Mrs Glasse's book does have the instruction 'Take your hare when it is cased [= skinned].' In more general terms, this appears to be a general formulation. The *Spirit of Farmers' Museum* (1801) has: 'How to dress a dolphin, first catch a dolphin.'

A source from a much earlier period, the medieval Latin treatise *De legibus et consuetudinibus Angliae*, traditionally attributed to the lawyer Henry of Bratton, has the sentence, 'It is commonly said that one must first catch the deer, and afterwards, when he has been caught, skin him.'

The fog of war

In 2004, *The Fog of War* was the title of Errol Morris's award-winning documentary about Robert S. McNamara, US Secretary of State during the Vietnam War. The phrase is now widely used in the context of a conflict which is not seen as clear cut. An article in the *Independent* of November 2005 on the methods used by American troops the year before in clearing Fallujah of insurgents was entitled, 'The fog of war: white phosphorus, Fallujah and some burning questions.'

The image is popularly associated with the Prussian soldier and military theorist Karl von Clausewitz, but rather than being a direct quotation, it seems to be a paraphrase. In *The Art of War* (1832–4), Clausewitz wrote: 'War is the realm of uncertainty; three quarters of the factors on which action in war is based are wrapped in a fog of greater or lesser uncertainty.'

Follow the money

In *All the President's Men*, the 1976 film depicting the unravelling of the Watergate conspiracy story by the *Washington Post* reporters Robert Woodward and Carl Bernstein, the mysterious source code-named 'Deep Throat' advises them to 'follow the money'. When, on 31 May 2005, an article in *Vanity Fair* revealed that the real 'Deep Throat' had been the former Deputy Director of the FBI, W. Mark Felt, nearly all the resulting coverage used or referred to the phrase as if it had been actually said by Felt to the reporters.

In an article 'Don't Follow the Money' in the *New York Times* of 12 June 2005, the columnist Frank Rich described a phone-call he had received from an old friend, William Goldman, screenwriter for *All the President's Men*. 'I wrote "Follow the money"', said Goldman, adding, 'I want to know if anyone will give me credit. Watch for the accuracy of the media!'

Noting that 'journalists everywhere—from *The New York Times* to *The Economist* to *The Washington Post* itself' did indeed attribute the line to Felt, Frank Rich suggested that the confusion of the film's reality with what really happened mirrors a particular feature of the Deep Throat coverage: was Felt a brave whistleblower or a treacherous (and perhaps disgruntled) employee, and should he (in Rich's words) be able to '"Follow the money" into a book deal.'

Frankly, my dear, I don't give a damn!

Famously spoken by Clark Gable, as Rhett Butler, to Vivien Leigh as Scarlett O'Hara, in the closing scene of the 1939 film of *Gone With the Wind*. The words have become iconic: the journalist Marina Hyde used them in a 2005 critique of Tony Blair's speech to the Labour Party Conference. Suggesting that key phrases failed to make any lasting impact, she quoted an extract, and gave the verdict 'Not exactly "Frankly my dear, I don't give a damn", is it?'

The precise wording was in fact the work of the screenwriter, Sidney Howard. In the 1936 novel by Margaret Mitchell, Rhett says to his wife, 'I wish I could care what you do or where you go but I can't…My dear, I don't give a damn.'

Fresh fields and pastures new

An expression of the desire to seek new areas of activity, which has become established in the language as a lexical item—as in, for example, a 1990s reference to 'corporate hopes for fresh fields and pastures new'. In James Joyce's *Ulysses*, the expression is seen as proverbial: 'As the adage has it, dreaming of fresh fields and pastures new.'

In the nineteenth century, references were more likely to indicate a consciousness of quotation origin, even if, as in the following passage from R. S. Surtees's *Handley Cross* (1854), the attribution is erroneous. Mr Jorrocks, discussing the unhappy state of a man forced to spend time in London society rather than in the country, says:

> No captive released from gaol—no bouy let free from school—no starlin' escaped from cage, hails with more 'eartfelt joy the arrival of that hour which restores him to wot the immortal Mr. Fieldin' (I thinks) calls 'Fresh fields and pastures new'.

The words derive ultimately from the closing lines of Milton's elegy *Lycidas* (1638):

> At last he rose, and twitched his mantle blue:
> Tomorrow to fresh woods, and pastures new.

The future is plastics

A catchphrase, implying a supposed vision of an exciting future which actually limits rather than inspires. The words are often quoted as a key line from the 1967 film *The Graduate*. The central character, Benjamin Braddock (played by Dustin Hoffman), is uncertain about what he is going to do now that he has graduated from college. In an early scene, he is told by a family friend, Mr McQuire, 'I want to say one word to you—just one word.' The word turns out to be 'plastics', and Mr McQuire amplifies, 'There's a great future in plastics.'

Genius is an infinite capacity for taking pains

A proverbial definition, often attributed to the Scottish historian and political philosopher Thomas Carlyle. However, the earliest record of the adage is found in J. E. Hopkins *Work Amongst Working Men* (1870). The nearest thing in Carlyle's work is a comment in his *History of Frederick the Great* (1858–65), 'Genius (which means transcendent capacity of taking trouble, first of all)'.

Germany is my spiritual home

In 1914, after the outbreak of war, a xenophobic press campaign was waged against the Minister of War, the Liberal politician Richard Burdon Haldane. Lord Haldane was said to have German sympathies, and the rumours received fresh impetus from accounts of a dinner given in 1913 by the novelist, Mrs Humphrey Ward, for Haldane to meet a number of German professors. At the dinner, Haldane had said that Professor Lötze's classroom in Göttingen was his spiritual home. The report spread that Haldane had claimed that 'Germany is my spiritual home.'

In the feverishly anti-German atmosphere of the time, the supposed comment was extremely harmful to Haldane. Asquith, the Prime Minister, although refusing his resignation at the time, dropped him from the Cabinet when forming a Coalition government in 1915.

Gild the lily

Over-embellish, especially in figurative use. The term is first recorded in the *Manchester Guardian Weekly* of September 1928: 'Nature and history have already been so kind to that ancient and charming townlet on the Dart that improvement would be a gilding of the lily.' The phrase comes ultimately from an alteration of a passage in Shakespeare's *King John*:

> To gild refined gold, to paint the lily,
> To throw a perfume on the violet,
> To smooth the ice, or add another hue
> Unto the rainbow, or with taper light
> To seek the beauteous eye of heaven to garnish,
> Is wasteful and ridiculous excess.

Git thar fustest with the mostest

Succinct advice attributed to the Confederate General Nathan Bedford Forrest, a representation of his saying as a Civil War cavalry leader, 'Get there first with the most men.' Hugh Rawson and Margaret Miner, in the *Oxford Dictionary of American Quotations* (2004), point out that there is no evidence that this kind of non-standard speech was characteristic of Forrest. Meanwhile the attribution is still found, although its dubious status is recognized. A *New York Times* article of May 1991, 'How to be the World's Policeman', reflects:

'Git thar fustest with the mostest'

> Increasingly, however, what makes conventional forces strategic is the ability, as the Confederate General Nathan Bedford Forrest supposedly put it, to 'git thar fustest with the mostest.'

God does not play dice

A statement which is often attributed in this form to Albert Einstein. What Einstein actually wrote, in a letter of 4 December 1926, to his fellow physicist Max Born, was:

> Quantum mechanics is certainly imposing. But an inner voice tells me that this is not yet the real thing. The theory says a lot, but does not bring us any closer to the secrets of the 'old one'. I, at any rate, am convinced that *He* [God] does not play dice.

Gold is a barbarous relic

A *Daily Telegraph* article of October 2002 noted that with a stock market depressed by the threat of war in Iraq, investors were increasingly turning to traditional commodities such as gold. Looking at how gold had performed, the verdict was given as 'a convincing revival for a commodity that several years ago was described as "a barbarous relic".' The reference was to an edict which in this form is widely attributed to the economist John Maynard Keynes.

The gold standard, a financial system by which the value of a currency was defined in terms of gold, had collapsed in most European countries as a result of the First World War, although it was reintroduced in Britain in 1925. Keynes was one of those who argued against its reintroduction: in his 1923 essay 'Alternative Aims in Monetary Policy' he wrote:

> In truth, the gold standard is already a barbarous relic. All of us, from the Governor of the Bank of England downwards, are now primarily interested in preserving the stability of business, prices, and employment, and are not likely, when the choice is forced on us, deliberately to sacrifice these to the outworn dogma, which had its value once, of £3.17.10½ per ounce. Advocates of the ancient standard do not observe how remote it now is from the spirit and requirements of the age. A regular non-metallic standard has slipped in unnoticed. *It exists*.

The good Christian should beware of mathematicians

A warning which comes from a mistranslation of St Augustine of Hippo's *De Genesi ad Litteram*. The mistranslation in full reads as follows:

> The good Christian should beware of mathematicians, and all those who make empty prophecies. The danger already exists that mathematicians have made a covenant with the Devil to darken the spirit and to confine man to the bonds of Hell.

The mistake derives from the Latin word *mathematicus* meaning both 'mathematician' and 'astrologer'. More correctly, the passage should be read:

> Hence, a devout Christian must avoid astrologers and all impious soothsayers, especially when they tell the truth, for fear of leading his soul into error by consorting with demons and entangling himself with the bonds of such an association.

A good day to bury bad news

A phrase which has now become so familiar that the final element may sometimes be varied. Kathryn Flett, in an *Observer* television review of June 2004, suggested that the scheduling of a particular item might have reflected a view about 'a good day to bury bad, albeit also quite expensive, drama.'

In the hours following news of the terrorist action in America on 11 September 2001 ('nine-eleven'), the British government adviser Jo Moore sent out an email reading, '**It is now a very good day to get out anything we want to bury. Councillors' expenses?**' This was leaked and widely reported; public shock and distaste were heightened by its becoming fixed in the general consciousness in the form, 'a good day to bury bad news'. In February 2002, when the *Daily Telegraph* reported that she had resigned from her position at the Department of Transport, the column was headed: '"A good day" for No 10 to bury Jo Moore's career.'

'A good day to bury bad news' may now be used to explain a less familiar term: a paragraph in *Risks Newsletter* (a weekly online bulletin issued by the Trades Union Congress) for December 2005 notes that 'In the US the day before a national holiday is known by the media as "take out the trash day", a good day to bury bad news.'

Go west, young man

In 1845, the American journalist John L. O'Sullivan had stated the principle of 'our manifest destiny to overspread the continent allotted by Providence for the free development of our yearly multiplying millions'. The concept of 'manifest destiny' forms a natural background to the injunction of a few years later, '**Go west, young man, and grow up with the country**', which appeared in a *New York Tribune* editorial.

The editorial was written by Horace Greeley, founder and editor of the paper, but as Hugh Rawson and Margaret Miner explain in the *Oxford Dictionary of American Quotations*, the formulation of 'Go west, young man' has traditionally been credited to another journalist, John B. L. Soule, editor of the *Terre Haute* (Indiana) *Express*. Greeley was thought to have reprinted an 1851 article by Soule as an editorial in the Tribune. However, recent researches in the archives of both papers have failed to find either the original article or the editorial reprinting it. Rawson and Miner conclude, therefore, that it is right to credit Greeley with the authorship 'since he often gave this advice, verbally and in print, though perhaps never exactly in these words'.

An association of the phrase in the public mind with Greeley is reinforced by a story of how the writer Nathanael West, born Nathan Weinstein, came to choose his pseudonym. Asked by William Carlos Williams how he had chosen the name 'West', he responded: '**Horace Greeley said, "Go West, young man." So I did.**'

Greater love hath no man than this, that he lay down his friends for his life

In March 2006, in the wake of a number of news stories about their financial affairs, it was announced that the Labour politician Tessa Jowell was separating from her husband. The *New York Sun*, reporting the story (including the verdict by the parliamentary commissioner for standards that no regulation about accurate declaration had been contravened by Tessa Jowell), went on to look at her role as a close political supporter and friend of Tony Blair. It concluded, 'Greater love hath no woman than this, who would lay down her marriage for her political friends.'

The mocking alteration of a biblical original is found forty years earlier in the world of British politics. In July 1962, in what became known as his 'night of the long knives', Harold Macmillan dismissed (or accepted the resignations of) the Chancellor of the Exchequer, Selwyn Lloyd, and six other Cabinet members. The Liberal politician Jeremy Thorpe commented bitingly, 'Greater love hath no man than this, that he lay down his friends for his life.' (Still earlier, James Joyce had written in *Ulysses* (1922), 'Greater love than this, he said, no man hath that a man lay down his wife for his friend.')

All these reworkings lead back to the dictum in St John's Gospel, in the Authorized Version translation of the Bible: 'Greater love hath no man than this, that a man lay down his life for his friends.'

The green shoots of recovery

Signs of growth or renewal which are taken as tokens of economic recovery. While 'green shoots' in this sense is recorded from the 1980s, the longer phrase is used especially in allusion to a speech of 1991 by Norman Lamont, then Chancellor of the Exchequer. Addressing the Conservative Party Conference in October 1991, the Chancellor said: 'The green shoots of economic spring are appearing once again.' This assessment (which later came to look somewhat over-optimistic) was transmuted into the phrase 'the green shoots of recovery'.

Gunpowder, printing, and the Protestant religion

In his essay 'The State of German Literature', Thomas Carlyle said that 'the three great elements of modern civilization' were 'Gunpowder, Printing, and the Protestant religion'. Carlyle was in fact borrowing from (and slightly altering the wording of) the English lawyer, philosopher, and essayist Francis Bacon. In his *Novum Organum* (1620), Bacon had written:

> It is well to observe the force and virtue and consequence of discoveries, and these are to be seen nowhere more conspicuously than in those three which were unknown to the ancients, and of which the origins, though recent, are obscure and inglorious; namely, printing, gunpowder, and the mariner's needle [compass]...these three have changed the whole face and state of things throughout the world.

Hamlet without the Prince

A phrase used to indicate a performance without the chief actor, or a proceeding without the central figure. An article in the *Independent* of December 2005, on the ceremony in Stockholm to present the Nobel Prize for Literature to Harold Pinter, described the company gathered on the podium as 'a head-spinningly distinguished throng of former laureates, members of the Nobel Academy, the Royal Swedish Science Academy, the Nobel Foundation, and some junior royals'. In addition, Lady Antonia Pinter with her children and grandchildren, and the American playwright Donald Freed, were in the stalls. However, Harold Pinter himself was absent—and 'without Harold Pinter in person, it was Hamlet without the Prince.'

'Hamlet without the Prince'

The phrase is an established one: in June 1910 the *Times Weekly* commented, 'The army without Kitchener is like Hamlet without the Prince of Denmark.' (The future of Lord Kitchener, the former commander-in-chief of the Army in India, was currently a matter of debate.) Nearly a century before, Lord Byron had written in a letter of August 1818, '**My autobiographical Essay would resemble the tragedy of Hamlet, recited "with the part of Hamlet left out by particular desire".**'

These and other references go back to a story recounted in the *Morning Post* of September 1775:

> *Lee Lewes* diverts them with the manner of their performing Hamlet in a company that he belonged to, when the hero who was to play the principal character had absconded with an inn-keeper's daughter, and that when he came forward to give out the play, he added, 'the part of Hamlet to be left out, for that night.'

Happiness is a warm –

There have been a number of variations on this theme. An early episode (November 1965) of the American sitcom set in a World War Two prisoner of war camp, *Hogan's Heroes*, was entitled '**Happiness is a warm sergeant.**' '**Happiness is a warm gun**' was the title of a song (1968) by the former Beatle John Lennon. An *Observer* column of September 2004 on the closure of a much-loved Somerset hotel was headed, '**Happiness is a warm bed...**'

Happiness is a Warm Puppy is the title of a best-selling book (1962) by the American cartoonist (and creator of *Peanuts*) Charles M. Schulz.

Hawking his conscience round the Chancelleries of Europe

In 1931 George Lansbury, the only former Labour cabinet minister who had survived the 1931 election, became leader of the Labour Party, then in opposition to the National Government of Ramsay Macdonald. His time in this role (1931–35) coincided with the rise of European fascism, and Lansbury's pacifist views put him at odds with other leading members of his party. The Abyssinian crisis of 1935, when Italy invaded Abyssinia, brought this to a head: at the Labour Party Conference of that year, Lansbury opposed a resolution condemning the invasion and calling for sanctions against Italy. It was widely said that the formidable Ernest Bevin taunted him in his reply for 'hawking his conscience round the Chancelleries of Europe'.

Reports of what Bevin actually said, although all cutting, in fact vary slightly. In the official report of the Labour Party Conference of 1935, Bevin's charge runs: 'It is placing the Executive and the Movement in an absolutely wrong position to be taking your conscience round from body to body asking to be told what to do with it.' John Shepherd, in his biography *George Lansbury* (2002), suggested that the official record toned down Bevin's words, and added that the *Observer* of the following weekend quoted the phrase 'hawking your conscience'. Other delegates agreed that this was what Bevin had said. Lansbury's granddaughter (who had been present), interviewed in 1989–90, recalled the key word as 'hawking', but also thought 'carting' a possibility.

Whatever the term used, the bitterness of the attack, and its destructive force, was not in doubt. After the Conference, Lansbury resigned the leadership of his Party.

A heartbeat away from the Presidency

The vice-presidency of the United States is popularly described as being 'Just a heartbeat away from the Presidency', since if a president dies in office, the vice-president succeeds him. A *Guardian* column of March 2004 considered the constitutional US chain of succession in the event of a president's death. The vice-president is 'a heartbeat away from the most powerful office in the world, and the speaker of the House and the president pro-tem of the Senate a heartbeat behind him.'

The formulation derives from a speech by the American politician

Adlai Stevenson during the US presidential campaign of 1952. In a reference to Richard Nixon, Republican candidate for the vice-presidency, he said scathingly:

> The Republican Party did not have to...encourage the excesses of its Vice-Presidential nominee—the young man who asks you to set him one heart-beat from the Presidency of the United States.

Hell hath no fury like a woman scorned

A proverbial view which was familiar in the Renaissance, and may reach back to the Furies in classical mythology, but which in this form derives from an alteration of lines in Congreve's 1697 play *The Mourning Bride*:

> Heaven has no rage, like love to hatred turned,
> Nor Hell a fury, like a woman scorned.

He once shot a publisher

The popular version of a reason given by the poet Thomas Campbell, at a literary dinner during the Napoleonic Wars, for proposing a toast to the Emperor Napoleon. The story is given in George Haven Puttnam's 1883 *Authors and Publishers: a manual of suggestions for beginners in literature*:

> The story of Campbell, at a literary dinner, proposing the health of Napoleon, because he 'once shot a publisher', has often been quoted as a fair expression of the feeling with which they regard each other, and if there is any truth in the picture which represents the publisher as a sort of ogre, whose den is strewn with the bones of authors, and who quaffs his wine out of their skulls, this assumption is certainly natural enough, as between the eater and the eaten there can be little love lost.

'He once shot a publisher'

The occasion is described in George Macaulay Trevelyan's *Life of Lord Macaulay* (1876). However, the original wording differs in one detail, looking back to the period when booksellers were also publishers (the *Oxford English Dictionary*, quoting from 1788 *Walpoliana*, refers to 'those booksellers in Paternoster-row who publish things in numbers'). According to Trevelyan (who described this as an anecdote which Macaulay 'told well and often, to illustrate the sentiment with which the authors of old days regarded their publishers'), Campbell's toast, addressed to his fellow authors, ran as follows:

> Gentleman, you must not mistake me. I admit that the French Emperor is a tyrant. I admit he is a monster. I admit he is the sworn foe of our nation, and, if you will, of the whole human race. But, gentlemen, we must be just to our great enemy. We must not forget that he once shot a bookseller.

He snatched the lightning shaft from heaven

The eighteenth-century French economist and politician Anne-Robert-Jacques Turgot, composed an inscription for the bust of Benjamin Franklin. In recognition of Franklin's invention of the lightning conductor as well as his role in achieving American independence, it ran: '*Eripuit coelo fulmen, sceptrumque tyrannis* [He snatched the lightning shaft from heaven, and the sceptre from tyrants].'

Turgot was reworking a classical original: lines by the Roman poet Manilius on human intelligence:

> *Eripuitque Jovi fulmen viresque tonandi*
> *Et sonitum ventis concessit, nubibus ignem.*

> [And snatched from Jove the lightning shaft and power to thunder, and attributed the noise to the winds, the flame to the clouds.]

He who hesitates is lost

A proverbial formulation, early uses of which specifically referred to women. Trollope's novel *Can You Forgive Her?* (1865) has, '**It has often been said of woman that she who doubts is lost.**' The maxim originates in a line by Addison in his play *Cato* (1713). In one scene, Cato's daughter Marcia, discussing her suitors with her friend Lucia, says:

> When love once pleads admission to our hearts
> (In spite of all the virtue we can boast)
> The woman that deliberates is lost.

Hold the fort! I am coming!

On 5 October 1864, the American Union General John Murray Corse was defending a crucial supply depot at Allatoona, in Georgia, against heavy Confederate attack. 'Hold the fort! I am coming!' is the popular version of a message sent to the beleaguered forces by Corse's superior, William Tecumseh Sherman. Sherman's actual signal ran, '**Hold out. Relief is coming.**' (Corse did hold out, and eventually the Confederates withdrew their attack.)

'Hold the fort! I am coming!' was given further currency by the words of Philip Paul Bliss's 1870 gospel song, 'Hold the Fort', which was inspired by the story. The refrain of the song runs:

> 'Hold the fort, for I am coming,' Jesus signals still;
> Wave the answer back to Heaven, 'By Thy grace we will.'

Homer sometimes nods

Proverbial acknowledgement that however great a person's capacities, they may still overlook something. Thomas Henry Huxley wrote in 1887 that 'Scientific reason, like Homer, sometimes nods', and Byron's poem *Don Juan* (1819-24) has: '**We learn from Horace, Homer sometimes sleeps.**' John Dryden, in the seventeenth century, commented, 'Horace acknowledges that honest Homer nods sometimes: he is not equally awake in every line.'

The reference is ultimately to a comment by the Roman poet Horace: '*Indignor quandoque bonus dormitat Homerus* [I am indignant when worthy Homer nods].'

An honest God is the noblest work of man

Robert Ingersoll, an American lawyer and orator, was the son of a Calvinist minister, but himself developed agnostic views. In January 1872, at a celebration in honour of the eighteenth-century radical Tom Paine, he delivered a lecture, 'The Gods', which made a direct attack on religion. The lecture began with the words '**An honest God is the noblest work of man.**'

Ingersoll was reworking the words of Pope in *An Essay on Man* (1734), '**An honest man's the noblest work of God**', later quoted by Burns in 'The Cotter's Saturday Night' (1786):

> Princes and lords are but the breath of kings,
> 'An honest man's the noblest work of God.'

A hundred guilty witches

In the autumn of 1692, a number of prominent clergymen interceded to stop the witchcraft trials, and executions, which since February of that year had been taking place in Salem, Massachusetts. One of these clergymen was the Puritan minister Increase Mather, who is often said to have expressed the view that it would be better for '**a hundred guilty witches to go free**', than for one innocent person to be condemned.

The sentiment is clearly in tune with what Mather believed, but what he actually wrote, in *Cases of Conscience Concerning Evil Spirits* (1692) was, '**It were better that ten suspected witches should escape, than that the innocent person should be condemned.**'

The intervention of Mather and his fellow clerics had a significant effect on public opinion, and contributed to bringing the trials to an end.

I am become Death, the destroyer of worlds

The *New York Times* of October 2005 carried a review of John Adams' opera 'Dr Atomic', an opera about the development of the atomic bomb. The review explains that the central character is the director of the project, Robert Oppenheimer, and quotes directly from him: '"I am become death, destroyer of worlds," Oppenheimer famously said when the first bomb went off.'

On 16 July 1945, the first atomic bomb was exploded near Alamagordo, New Mexico. The American physicist J. Robert Oppenheimer, director of the laboratory at Los Alamos where it had been built, who witnessed it, said later: 'I remembered the line from the Hindu scripture, the Bhagavad Gita..."I am become death, the destroyer of worlds."'

Oppenheimer was in fact slightly misquoting the epic Hindu poem. In the dialogue between the Kshatriya prince Arjuna and his divine charioteer Krishna, the god says:

> I am all-powerful Time which destroys all things, and I have come here to slay these men. Even if thou doest not fight, all the warriors facing thee shall die.

I am the American

Words which are frequently attributed to Mark Twain, and which appear in a notebook compiled by him in the summer of 1897.

'I am the American'

The notebook contains a number of descriptions and comments attributed to Twain's friend Frank Fuller. The key page opens with a statement attributed to Fuller which indicates that he thinks people he meets at a hotel are trying to steal his watch. The question is asked 'Are you an American?'

to which either Fuller or an unidentified person replies: 'No. I am not an American. I am *the* American.'

I disapprove of what you say, but I will defend to the death your right to say it

A column in the *Daily Telegraph* of February 2006 on freedom of speech referred to 'Voltaire's famous maxim—"I disapprove of what you say, but I will defend to the death your right to say it."'

In *De l'esprit* ['On the Mind'], published in 1758, the French philosopher Helvétius put forward the view that human motivation derives from sensation: a course of action is chosen because of the pleasure or pain which will result. The book was seen by many as an attack on religion and morality, and was condemned by the French parliament to be publicly burned. Voltaire is supposed to have supported Helvétius with these words. In fact, they are a later summary of Voltaire's attitude to the affair, as given in S. G. Tallentyre's *The Friends of Voltaire* (1907). What Tallentyre wrote was:

> What the book could never have done for itself, or for its author, persecution did for them both. 'On the Mind' became not the success of a season, but one of the most famous books of the century. The men who had hated it, and had not particularly loved Helvétius, flocked round him now. Voltaire forgave him all injuries, intentional or unintentional. 'What a fuss about an omelette!' he had exclaimed when he heard of the burning. How abominably unjust to persecute a man for such an airy trifle as that! 'I disapprove of what you say, but I will defend to the death your right to say it,' was his attitude now.

(The comment 'What a fuss about an omelette!' had been recorded earlier, in James Parton's 1881 *Life of Voltaire*.)

I don't know what effect these men will have upon the enemy, but, by God, they frighten me

A comment now often used when writing about a group which should be counted as a support, but which is seen as inherently alarming even to those on the same side.

In 2004, a reviewer of Anthony Swofford's *Jarhead*, an account of an American Marine's time in Kuwait in the first Gulf War, wrote: 'As I read, I kept recalling the Duke of Wellington's words; I don't know what effect these men will have upon the enemy, but, by God, they frighten me.'

This is the usual form in which the Duke of Wellington's assessment of his army is quoted. What Wellington actually wrote, in a letter of 29 August 1810, was: 'As Lord Chesterfield said of the generals of his day, "I only hope that when the enemy reads the list of their names, he trembles as I do."'

If I can't dance, I don't want to be in your revolution

A statement attributed to the Lithuanian-born American feminist and revolutionary Emma Goldman. In fact, as Alix Kates Shulman, editor of *Dancing in the Revolution: Selected Writings and Speeches of Emma Goldman* (1983) has explained, the words are a summary of what Goldman believed, rather than a direct quotation from what she said or wrote. In her autobiography *Living my Life* (1931), Emma Goldman noted that at dances she was 'one of the most untiring and gayest', but was told by a fellow revolutionary that 'it did not behoove an agitator to dance.' Telling her critic to mind his own business, she added that:

> I was tired of having the Cause constantly thrown into my face. I did not believe that a Cause which stood for a beautiful ideal, for anarchism, for release and freedom from conventions and prejudice, should demand

the denial of life and joy. I insisted that our Cause could not expect me to become a nun and that the movement should not be turned into a cloister. If it meant that, I did not want it. 'I want freedom, the right to self-expression, everybody's right to beautiful, radiant things.'

I forgot to duck

In 1981, President Ronald Reagan was shot and wounded in an assassination attempt by John Hinckley. Afterwards, he joked to his wife Nancy, '**Honey, I forgot to duck.**'

Reagan was reworking a famous comment by the American boxer Jack Dempsey. Dempsey, defending his World Heavyweight title, was defeated by Gene Tunney on 23 September 1926. Afterwards, Dempsey explained to his wife, '**Honey, I just forgot to duck.**'

If the glove doesn't fit, you must acquit

In June 2004, a report on Networkworld.com carried the heading '**SCO's case doesn't fit, but the lawyers won't quit.**'

During the trial (1994–6) of O. J. Simpson for the murder of his wife Nicole and Ronald Goldman, the Prosecution's case included a pair of bloodstained gloves. These, when tried on by Simpson, appeared not to fit, something which was taken up to great effect by Simpson's defence counsel, Johnnie Cochran. Cochran told the jury, '**If it doesn't fit, you must acquit.**'

O. J. Simpson was acquitted, and the altered refrain 'If the glove doesn't fit, you must acquit' was widely quoted when describing his successful defence. In the *New York Times* article of March 2005 which announced Johnnie Cochran's death, it was noted that Cochran himself grew tired of the line's place in popular culture. He is quoted as saying: '**It's...the line endlessly quoted to me by people, the line by which I'll be remembered, and I suspect it will probably be my epitaph.**'

If we are not for ourselves, then who will be with us?

A modification, now frequently quoted, of the first-century Jewish scholar and teacher Hillel the Elder. Hillel's original words, recorded in the Talmud, are, 'If I am not for myself who is for me? And being for my own self what am I? If not now when?'

If you build it, they will come

An article in the *New York Times* for February 2006 gave an account of the 1930s attempt to turn Yosemite National Park into a major ski centre for West Coast America. The article described the particularly well-built ski lodge that was erected in 1941, but went on: 'The maxim "If you build it, they will come" did not hold true. In its first winter, the hut drew 154 skiers.' After the war, with the popularity of downhill skiing rising, other resorts were developed. In the film *Field of Dreams* (1989), the hero, an Iowa farmer (Ray Kinsella, played by Kevin Costner), lays out a baseball diamond in the middle of one of his cornfields, after hearing a voice that tells him, 'If you build it, he will come.' ('He' is the baseball star 'Shoeless' Joe Jackson, who does indeed appear on the cornfield diamond.) Other spirits from baseball's past appear in response to the farmer's dream, and 'If you build it, they will come' has become a saying that endorses the possibility of following one's dreams.

> 'If you build it, they will come'

If you cannot measure it, then it is not science

A view which is often attributed to the British mathematician and physicist Lord Kelvin, known for introducing the absolute scale of temperature. The single sentence is actually the summary of the thought in a much longer passage, from a lecture delivered in May 1883:

> When you cannot measure what you are speaking about, and express it in numbers, you know something about it; but when you cannot measure it, when you cannot express it in numbers, your knowledge is of a meager and unsatisfactory kind: it may be the beginning of knowledge, but you have scarcely, in your thoughts, advanced to the stage of science, whatever the matter may be.

If you can't ride two horses at once, you shouldn't be in the circus

A modern saying about the minimum capability needed for a particular role. It appears to derive from a protest by the Labour politician James Maxton against the proposal, in 1931, to disaffiliate the Scottish Labour Party from the Labour Party. Maxton is reported in the *Daily Herald* of 12 January 1931 as saying, 'All I say is, if you cannot ride two horses you have no right in the circus.' He is often quoted as saying, more strongly, 'no right in the bloody circus'.

If you haven't got anything good to say about anyone come and sit by me

A tart saying attributed to President Theodore Roosevelt's witty daughter Alice Roosevelt Longworth. In fact, as Michael Teague recounts in his 1981 book *Mrs L: Conversations with Alice Roosevelt Longworth*, it was actually a maxim embroidered on a cushion in her home.

I had hoped that liberal and enlightened thought would have reconciled the Christians

A comment now frequently attributed in this form to George Washington. It appears to be an alteration of a passage in a letter of June 1792, discussing religious friction:

> Religious controversies are always productive of more acrimony and irreconcilable hatreds than those which spring from any other cause; and I was not without hopes that the enlightened and liberal policy of the present age would have put an effectual stop to contentions of this kind.

I have gazed upon the face of Agamemnon

Words attributed to the German archaeologist Heinrich Schliemann. They are sometimes used as the type of a significant discovery, as in a *Daily Telegraph* column of May 2003: 'There is nothing more exciting for an editor than to see the original material which produced a scoop. I feel like Schliemann when he discovered Mycenae: "I have gazed on the face of Agamemnon."' In 1876, Schliemann had unearthed a number of gold grave goods in his excavation of a Greek Bronze Age site at Mycenae. The discovery included three bodies, wearing gold masks. With one of the bodies, when the gold mask was removed, Schliemann said that 'The round face, with all its flesh, had been wonderfully preserved under its ponderous golden mask.'

J. Lesley Fitton, in her book *The Discovery of the Greek Bronze Age* (1995), says that this was the body 'that Schliemann liked to think was that of Agamemnon', although she points out that the mask it wore was 'relatively unimpressive', and was not the fine one which 'is often, though wrongly, referred to as the Mask of Agamemnon'. She confirms that the story of his sending a telegram claiming that 'Today I have gazed upon the face of Agamemnon' is apocryphal.

> The nearest equivalent—and it is nothing like so dramatic or romantic— seems to be his comment in a telegram to the Greek press: 'This corpse

very much resembles the image which my imagination formed long ago of wide-ruling Agamemnon.'

I never loved a dear gazelle

In Charles Dickens's *The Old Curiosity Shop* (1841), Dick Swiveller laments that: 'I never loved a dear Gazelle, to glad me with its soft black eye, but when it came to know me well and love me, it was sure to marry a market-gardener.'

He was making a humorous reference to lines from the popular *Lalla Rookh* (1817), the story (told in verse with linking prose) of the marriage journey of the daughter of the Emperor of India, by the Irish musician and songwriter Thomas Moore. The relevant lines were:

> I never nursed a dear gazelle,
> To glad me with its soft black eye,
> But when it came to know me well,
> And love me, it was sure to die!

Moore's lines were later parodied by Lewis Carroll, in a poem beginning:

> I never loved a dear Gazelle—
> Nor anything that cost me much.

The sentimental image of the gazelle as a pet to nurture seems to have been popular in the nineteenth century: The poet Thomas Haynes Bayly in his 'Something to Love' (1844) had:

> Some tame gazelle, or some gentle dove:
> Something to love. Oh, something to love!

(Lines which in the mid twentieth century were to provide the novelist Barbara Pym with a title and an epigraph.)

An inn where all are received

An extract from a longer passage, which since 2003 has appeared as an attribution to the sixteenth-century English theologian and clergyman Richard Hooker. The passage in full reads: 'Pray that none will be offended if I seek to make the Christian Religion an inn where all are received joyously, rather than a cottage where some few friends or the family are to be received.' However, it does not appear that either the shorter or the longer version have been traced in Hooker's works.

An inordinate fondness for beetles

According to a popular story, the Scottish mathematical biologist J. B. S. Haldane was asked what his studies of nature might show about God. Haldane is supposed to have replied, 'An inordinate fondness for beetles.'

The story goes back to notes of a lecture given by Haldane in 1951. In April 1951, he gave a talk to the British Interplanetary Society entitled 'Biological Problems of Space Flight'. From the report published in the Society's *Journal*, this was 'an informal talk, which was not only most interesting but also witty and highly entertaining'. On the question of life being found on other planets, he dealt first with the hypothesis that life had a supernatural origin—a hypothesis, he said, which should be taken seriously.

> From the fact that there are 400,000 species of beetle on this planet, but only 8,000 species of mammals, he concluded that the Creator, if he exists, has a special preference for beetles, and so we might be more likely to meet them than any other type of animal on a planet which would support life.

Instead of rocking the cradle, they rocked the system

In November 1990, Mary Robinson was elected as President of Ireland, the first woman to hold that office. In her victory speech, paying tribute to the women of Ireland, she said, '**Instead of rocking the cradle, they rocked the system.**'

Mary Robinson was alluding to the proverbial saying, 'The hand that rocks the cradle rules the world.' It comes originally from a poem by the nineteenth-century American lawyer and poet William Ross Wallace. In 'The Hand that Rules the World', Wallace wrote:

> A mightier power and stronger
> Man from his throne has hurled,
> For the hand that rocks the cradle
> Is the hand that rules the world.

In trust I have found treason

The traditional concluding words of a speech by Queen Elizabeth I given to her Parliament in 1586, as printed in Camden's *Annals*:

> As for me, I see no such great cause why I should either be fond to live or fear to die. I have had good experience of this world, and I know what it is to be a subject and what to be a sovereign. Good neighbours I have had, and I have met with bad: and in trust I have found treason.

'In trust I have found treason'

The historian John Neale, in *Elizabeth I and her Parliaments 1584–1601* (1957), published what appears to be the authoritative version of this, working from a report 'which the Queen herself heavily amended in her own hand'. Her actual words according to this text were:

> As for me, I assure you I find no great cause I should be fond to live. I take no such pleasure in it that I should much will it, nor conceive such terror in death that I should greatly fear it...I have had good experience

and trial of this world. I know what it is to be a subject, what to be a Sovereign, what to have good neighbours, and sometimes meet evil-willers.

I rob banks because that's where the money is

'Fraud Busting Begins at Home', an article on fraud in the *New York Times* of January 2006, commented that ' For the same reason that Willie Sutton famously robbed banks, big-money schemes aim at Medicaid and other state health care programs.'

The reference was to an explanation for his motives frequently attributed, in this form, to the American bank robber Willie Sutton, nicknamed 'the Actor'. He was said to have been asked why he robbed banks, and to have responded 'because that's where the money is'. The *American National Biography*, calling this 'the most familiar quotation in American criminal history', notes that 'Sutton later denied having made the remark, but he was astute enough to know that in the business of newspaper headlines a good legend beats the truth every day.' His autobiography, published in 1976, was entitled *Where the Money Was*.

Is that a pistol in your pocket, or are you just glad to see me?

Popular version of Mae West's question 'Is that a gun in your pocket, or are you just pleased to see me?' Hugh Rawson and Margaret Miner, in the *Oxford Dictionary of American Quotations*, note that while this was one of her most famous lines, it did not occur in a film until the 1978 *Sextette*. (The screenplay of which, written by Herbert Baker, was based on a play by Mae West.)

The line is now so much part of the general vocabulary, that the words 'or are you just pleased to see me?' can be preceded by a wide number of variants. The dashing Lord Flashheart in 'Bells', the first episode of Ben Elton and Richard Curtis's *Blackadder II* (1986),

recasts it to greet the Queen's Nurse with the words, 'Am I pleased to
see you or did I just put a canoe in my pocket?'

It is impossible to rightly govern the world without God and the Bible

An assertion which has been frequently attributed to George
Washington, but which has never been traced in records of
his speech or writings. Paul F. Boller Jr. and John George, in *They
Never Said It* (1983), point out that while Washington (an Anglican)
attended church regularly and 'believed that religion was the
foundation for morality', he rarely mentioned the Bible. A reference
in notes for one of his speeches to 'the blessed Religion revealed in
the word of God' did not appear in the final version of the speech.

It is necessary only for the good man to do nothing for evil to triumph

A review in the *Observer* of September 2004 of Ronan Bennett's
novel *Havoc in its Third Year* is headed 'A good man in a time
of terror'. The reference, as the review makes clear, is to a saying
credited to Burke: 'For evil to triumph, it is necessary only for good
men to do nothing.'

The view, in varying forms, is widely attributed to the Whig
politician and man of letters Edmund Burke. It has never been
traced in his writings, and probably represents a summary of his
thoughts; for example, in his *Thoughts on the Present Discontents* (1770):
'When bad men combine, the good must associate; else they will fall,
one by one, an unpitied sacrifice in a contemptible struggle.'

It's a funny old world

In November 1990, Margaret Thatcher received the advice from the majority of her Cabinet that she would lose the Conservative leadership election, and therefore could not continue as Prime Minister. Accepting the advice (which she was later to characterize as 'treachery with a smile on its face'), she formally withdrew from the leadership contest. However, reflecting that as Party Leader she had never lost a general election, she commented ruefully, 'It's a funny old world').

The words were borrowed from a much earlier, and very different, source. In the 1934 film *You're Telling Me*, the character played by W. C. Fields comments, 'It's a funny old world—a man's lucky if he gets out of it alive.'

It's life, Jim, but not as we know it

In October 2004, a *Guardian* column reporting a new advertising campaign by McDonald's was headed, 'McDonald's ads. But not as you know them.' The text went on to say that McDonald's new advertising slogan, 'McDonald's. But not as you know it' was a play on Mr Spock's supposed reply to Captain Kirk in the *Star Trek* series, 'It's Life, Jim, but not as we know it.'

Although in one episode Mr Spock does refer to 'no life as we know it', the version now as characteristic comes instead from a 1987 song 'Star Trekkin'', sung by The Firm.

It's not the voting that's democracy, it's the counting

A line from Tom Stoppard's 1972 play *Jumpers*. The fictional assertion echoes a real-life formulation: the reported reply of the Nicaraguan dictator Anastasio Somoza responding to an allegation of vote-rigging: 'You won the elections, but I won the count.' It is also very close to a comment widely attributed (although without a specific source) to Joseph Stalin, 'Those who vote decide nothing. Those who count the votes decide everything.'

I used to be the next President

In the autumn of 2000, Al Gore, then Vice-President of the United States and Democratic nominee for the presidency, was defeated in the presidential election by George W. Bush. In the following March, he introduced himself to a student audience with the words, 'I am Al Gore, and I used to be the next President of the United States.' The introduction held a wry allusion to the words of an earlier (and more successful) presidential candidate. In November 1975, Jimmy Carter had told the young son of one of his supporters, 'I'm Jimmy Carter, and I'm going to be your next President.'

I want to be alone

A line which has long been regarded as the trademark utterance of the actress Greta Garbo, although she herself asserted (in *Life Magazine*, 1955), that she 'only said, "I want to be let alone!"' As Nigel Rees has pointed out in *Brewer's Quotations* (1994), she did have the line in several films. In the earliest of these, the silent *The Single Standard* (1929), the subtitle runs 'I am walking alone because I want to be alone.' Famously, she spoke it in *Grand Hotel* (1932), as the ballerina Grusinskaya, to her would-be lover the Baron von Gaigern (John Barrymore). (She finally conceded, 'For just a minute, then.') Alexander Walker, in *The Celluloid Sacrifice: Aspects of Sex in the Movies* (1966), confirmed that there is no record of 'I want to be alone' in any interview, although variants like 'Why don't you let me alone?' and 'I want to be left alone' can be found.

> **'I want to be alone'**

The line, and its association with Garbo, was clearly well-known by 1930. In that year, the humorous writers W. C. Sellar and R. J.

Yeatman published *Garden Rubbish*. The punning chapter headings, consisting of supposed quotations, included, '"**I want to be a lawn.**" **Greta Garbo**.' Two years later, as noted by Barry Paris in his 1995 biography *Garbo*, Marion Davies and Jimmy Durante parodied the Garbo-Barrymore love scene from *Grand Hotel*. In *Blondie of the Follies*, Davies said '**I vant to be alone**', and then conceded that after she would accept Durante's company for a limited period: 'Vell, maybe for a veek.'

Justice delayed is justice denied

A saying which in this form is not recorded before the late twentieth century. (It is however worth noting that in 1928 the American poet Edna St Vincent Millay gave the title 'Justice Denied in Massachusetts' to her poem on the controversial trial and execution of the anarchists Sacco and Vanzetti.)

The idea of a link between the delay and the denial of justice goes back to a much earlier original. A clause of the Magna Carta, the charter signed by King John at Runnymede in 1215, reads: '*Nulli vendemus, nulli negabimus aut differemus, rectum aut justitiam* [To no man will we sell, or deny, or delay, right of justice].'

Justify the ways of God to man

The geneticist Steve Jones, in a *Daily Telegraph* column of July 2005, wrote that: 'Malt says more than Milton can to justify God's ways to man, and yeast, the stuff that helps in that theological task, has had its ways much justified by systems scientists.' Immediately, he was quoting (or slightly misquoting) a couplet from A.E. Housman's poem *A Shropshire Lad* (1896):

And malt does more than Milton can
To justify God's ways to man.

However, Housman's lines themselves are part allusion, part

misquotation. The reference is to a passage in the first book of
Milton's *Paradise Lost* (1667):

> What in me is dark,
> Illumine, what is low raise and support;
> That to the height of this great argument
> I may assert eternal providence,
> And justify the ways of God to men.

The lady's not for turning

In her speech to the Conservative Party Conference in October
1980, Margaret Thatcher, who had become Prime Minister in
the previous year, told her audience: 'To those waiting with bated
breath for that favourite media catchphrase, the U-turn, I have
only this to say: "You turn if you want; the lady's not for turning."'
The punchline, 'the lady's not for turning', reworked the title of
Christopher Fry's 1949 play, *The Lady's Not for Burning*.

Ronald Millar, Margaret Thatcher's speechwriter, described
the genesis of the key line (which he referred to as TLNFT) in his
1993 autobiography, *A View from the Wings*. He was working on Mrs
Thatcher's Conference speech with the head of the Number Ten
Policy Unit, John Hoskyns, and together they were looking for
something to fit a headline space. It had to be 'not too short, not too
long, crisp and easily remembered for maybe an hour or so or even,
hopefully, a day or two'. When Millar came up with the line, they
decided to try it, but Millar noted that he was neutral about it (and
wondered if the play title would be remembered). He thought that
if the media 'went for it' they would pick up the 'U-turn' part—but
they went for 'the lady's not for turning', and 'they were right'. Millar
added:

> TLNFT has stood the test of time precisely because it's not a one-liner. In
> itself it's quite unremarkable, but it sprang freshly minted out of the text
> and caught on because it pinned the lady's character down in five short
> words. It *was* Thatcher and was instantly seen to be her by the public.

Laws are like sausages. It's better not to see them being made

A comment popularly attributed to the German statesman Otto von Bismarck (1815–98). (The precise form may vary, as for instance 'If you like laws and sausage, you should never watch either being made.') No source for the quotation, however, has been traced. In more recent online sources it has frequently been attributed to Winston Churchill.

Lead on, Macduff

In the final scene of Shakespeare's *Macbeth*, Macbeth, brought to bay by the wronged Macduff, challenges his enemy and nemesis to fight in the last words he speaks in the play:

> Lay on, Macduff;
> And damned be him that first cries, 'Hold, enough!'

'Lead on, Macduff'

The first three words have given rise to a humorous alteration, as in Rider Haggard's *King Solomon's Mines* (1885):

> 'Are ye prepared to enter the Place of Death?' asked Gagool, evidently with a view to making us feel uncomfortable. 'Lead on, Macduff,' said Good solemnly, trying to look as though he was not at all alarmed.

The leopard does not change his spots

A statement of the impossibility of change in someone's essential character, which has become proverbial. Recorded from the mid 16th century, an allusion to it is found in Shakespeare's *Richard II* (1596), when in response to the king's 'Lions make leopards tame' Mowbray retorts, 'Yea, but not change his spots.' The origin of the proverb is found in the Bible (from the translation of the Authorized

Version), in Jeremiah 13:23, 'Can the Ethiopian change his skin, or the leopard his spots?'

Let the boy win his spurs

A popular summary of the words of Edward III (1312–77) of his son, the Black Prince, at the battle of Crécy, in 1346. According to Froissart's *Chronicle*, the King said:

> Also say to them, that they suffer hym this day to wynne his spurres, for if god be pleased, I woll this journey be his, and the honoure therof. (*The Chronicle of Froissart*, translated by Sir John Bourchier, Lord Berners, 1523-5, ch. 130.)

Spurs were one of the traditional accoutrements of a knight, and to *win one's spurs* was to gain a knighthood through an act of bravery.

Let them eat cake

A letter in the *New York Times Magazine* of March 2006 opens: 'There is a certain "let them eat cake" aspect to the anti-zoning view. Almost no one with money, despite the rhetoric, is actually against zoning.'

'Let them eat cake', which is now the type of a dismissive comment redolent of carelessness and ignorance, is popularly (and slanderously) attributed to Marie Antoinette, Queen of France, on being told that her people had no bread. A passage of dialogue in Fay Weldon's *Darcy's Utopia* (1990) gives a good picture of common usage:

> 'And they have such long holidays! Why can't they do two jobs, if they're short of money?' 'Let them eat cake,' murmured Freddie. 'I never understood why poor Marie Antoinette got such stick for saying that,' said Eleanor. 'It seems a perfectly good suggestion to me, though cake's not very good for you.'

Marie Antoinette's biographer Antonia Fraser, writing of the time in 1774 known as the 'Flour War', when a disastrous harvest was succeeded by grain riots, said:

> Now, if at all, during the period of the Flour War, was the occasion when Marie Antoinette might have uttered the notorious phrase 'Let them eat cake' (*Qu'ils mangent de la brioche*). Instead, she indulged to her mother in a piece of reflection on the duties of royalty. Its tenor was the exact opposite of that phrase, at once callous and ignorant, so often ascribed to her. 'It is quite certain,' she wrote, 'that in seeing the people who treat us so well despite their own misfortune, we are more obliged than ever to work hard for their happiness.'

The phrase is in fact much earlier: Rousseau, in his *Confessions* (1740) refers to a similar remark as a well-known saying. Another version, 'Why don't they eat pastry?' is attributed in the memoirs of Marie Antoinette's brother-in-law (later Louis XVIII), published in 1823, to an earlier Queen of France, the Spanish princess Marie Thérèse, wife of Louis XIV. Nevertheless, in the general vocabulary the phrase remains inextricably linked with Marie Antoinette.

A lie is an abomination unto the Lord

The American politician Adlai Stevenson is quoted in Bill Adler's 1966 *The Stevenson Wit* as saying: 'It reminds me of the small boy who jumbled his biblical quotations and said, "A lie is an abomination unto the Lord, and a very present help in trouble."'

That this was in fact a well-established blend is shown by Hugh Rawson and Margaret Miner in the *Oxford Dictionary of American Quotations* (2004). They point out that a similar comment, 'A lie is an abomination unto the Lord and an ever present help in time of need', is attributed to John A. Morgan in the United States Senate, c.1890, by a 1977 account of the building of the Panama Canal, David McCullough's *The Path Between the Seas*.

The 'biblical' verses referred to are, respectively, 'Lying lips are an abomination to the Lord' from the book of Proverbs, and 'God is our refuge: a very present help in trouble' from the Psalms.

It is interesting to note that the concept of a necessary lie was defended in 1862 by the Conservative statesman (and future Prime Minister) Lord Salisbury: 'No one is fit to be trusted with a secret who is not prepared, if necessary, to tell an untruth to defend it.'

Life is not meant to be easy

Words used by the Australian Liberal statesman (and future Prime Minister) Malcolm Fraser when giving the fifth Alfred Deakin Lecture in July 1971. (Alfred Deakin was Prime Minister of Australia in the first decade of the twentieth century.) Fraser took the adjuration from a longer sentence by George Bernard Shaw. In Shaw's play *Back to Methuselah* (rev. edn, 1930), the He-Ancient says to Strephon, 'Life is not meant to be easy, my child; but take courage: it can be delightful.'

A little knowledge is a dangerous thing

An alteration, which has become proverbial, of lines in *An Essay on Criticism* (1711) by Alexander Pope.

> A little learning is a dangerous thing;
> Drink deep, or taste not the Pierian spring.
> There shallow draughts intoxicate the brain,
> And drinking largely sobers us again.

The first use of 'knowledge' rather than 'learning' is found in the late 19th century, as in the following comment by the biologist Thomas Henry Huxley in his essay 'On Elementary Instruction in Physiology': 'If a little knowledge is dangerous, where is the man who has so much as to be out of danger?'

Look out, gentlemen—the schoolmaster is abroad!

A warning said to have been given by the nineteenth-century lawyer and politician Lord Brougham in a speech at the Mechanics' Institute, London, in 1825. Brougham had become involved in the Mechanics Institutes (set up by his friend George Birkbeck) in 1824, and he subsequently encouraged the formation of further Institutes throughout the country.

A more formal version of Brougham's words is recorded in Hansard's record for the House of Commons, 29 January 1828:

> The schoolmaster is abroad! And I trust more to the schoolmaster, armed with his primer, than I do to the soldier in full military array, for upholding and extending the liberties of his country.

The expression entered the language: by the end of the nineteenth century, Oscar Wilde used it ironically, with a play on 'abroad', in *The Critic as Artist* (1891):

> People say that the schoolmaster is abroad. I wish to goodness he were. But the type of which, after all, he is only one, and certainly the least important, of the representatives, seems to me to be really dominating our lives; and just as the philanthropist is the nuisance of the ethical sphere, so the nuisance of the intellectual sphere is the man who is so occupied in trying to educate others, that he has never had any time to educate himself.

Make the trains run on time

That his administration 'made the trains run on time' was traditionally said to be the one favourable comment to be made about the Italian Fascist Benito Mussolini as Dictator of Italy. There is no contemporary record of this summary, although the following account by a Spanish princess, the Infanta Eulalia, published in 1925, confirms that an improvement in the rail service was noticed:

'Make the trains run on time'

The first benefit of Benito Mussolini's direction in Italy begins to be felt when one crosses the Italian Frontier and hears '*Il treno arriva all'orario* [The train is arriving on time].'

A later source, Giorgio Pini's *Mussolini* (1939) quotes Mussolini himself as saying to a station-master, '**We must leave exactly on time...From now on everything must function to perfection.**'

It is interesting to note that in the Indian setting of Salman Rushdie's 1981 novel *Midnight's Children*, the accurate running of trains is also seen to reflect the state of the country: '**All sorts of things happen during an Emergency: trains run on time, black-money hoarders are frightened into paying taxes.**'

Man, if you gotta ask, you'll never know

An alternative (and much quoted) version of the response given by the American singer and jazz musician Louis Armstrong when asked what jazz was. In *Salute to Satchmo* (1970) by Max Jones et al., the form given is, '**If you still have to ask...shame on you.**'

Man's love is of man's life a thing apart

In his poem 'A Bookshop Idyll' (1956), the writer Kingsley Amis reflected:

> Man's love is of man's life a thing apart;
> Girls aren't like that.

This was a mid-twentieth-century reworking of an original from the early nineteenth century: Byron's *Don Juan* (1819–24):

> Man's love is of man's life a thing apart,
> 'Tis woman's whole existence.

Me Tarzan, you Jane

In *Tarzan of the Apes* (1914), first of a series of novels by the American writer Edgar Rice Burroughs, Tarzan (Lord Greystoke by birth) is orphaned in West Africa in his infancy and reared by apes in the jungle. '**Me Tarzan, you Jane**' are supposedly the words with which Tarzan introduced himself to his future wife, Jane Porter. In fact, they were first used by the Olympic swimming champion Johnny Weissmuller, in *Photoplay Magazine*, summing up his role as Tarzan in the 1932 film *Tarzan of the Apes*. The words do not occur in the film itself, nor in the original book by Burroughs.

The words are now sometimes used allusively, as in an extract from *An Eye for the Future*, May 1998: '**We find ourselves attracted, sometimes mildly, sometimes intensely, to all kinds of people of both sexes who seem to have nothing to do with our primitive 'Me Tarzan, you Jane' needs for survival.**'

Mind has no sex

A statement taken as summarizing the views of the English feminist Mary Wollstonecraft, as expressed in her *A Vindication of the Rights of Woman* (1792): '**To give a sex to mind was not very consistent with the principles of a man [Rousseau] who argued so warmly, and so well, for the immortality of the soul.**'

The actual form of the words is found not in Wollstonecraft's writings, but in a novel, *Anna St Ives*, by Thomas Holcroft, published in the same year. In one scene, a young lady challenges her lover:

> Dare you receive a blow, or suffer yourself to be called falsely liar, or coward, without seeking revenge, or what honour calls satisfaction? Dare you think the servant that cleans your shoes is your equal, unless not so wise or good a man; and your superior, if wiser and better? Dare you suppose that mind has no sex, and that woman is not by nature the inferior of man?

Monkeys on typewriters

In March 2006, it was reported that *I Bet You Look Good on the Dancefloor* by the Arctic Monkeys was currently in the lead in the search for the greatest pop lyric of all time. A *Times* leader on the topic, which showed some skepticism at the choice, was headed 'Monkeys with typewriters'.

The heading looked back to an image from the first part of the twentieth century. The British astrophysicist Arthur Eddington had commented dryly in *The Nature of the Physical World* (1928) that 'If an army of monkeys were strumming on typewriters they *might* write all the books in the British museum.'

The image was picked up in 1997 by the American academic Robert Wilensky, and given a sardonic twist: 'We've all heard that a million monkeys banging on a million typewriters will eventually reproduce the entire works of Shakespeare. Now, thanks to the Internet, we know this is not true.'

The most beautiful adventure

The last recorded words of the theatrical producer and director Charles Frohman, who was drowned when the Lusitania was sunk by enemy action in 1915, were, 'Why fear death? It is the most beautiful adventure in life.'

Frohman had been a friend of the Scottish writer and dramatist J. M. Barrie, and his words have an echo of a line in Barrie's *Peter Pan*: 'To die will be an awfully big adventure.'

The Mother of Parliaments

Often now used as a name for the British Houses of Parliament. A character in Isabel Colegate's 1988 novel *Deceits of Time* says: 'I believe I am the happiest man I know. I believe in God and in the institution which I serve, the Mother of Parliaments.' The first recorded use in this sense comes from the *Daily Mirror* of 12 November 1918, the day after the ending of the First World War: 'Never has the Mother of Parliaments seen such a scene of enthusiasm as when Mr Lloyd George read out the armistice terms yesterday.'

The name goes back to a speech of 1865 by the English Liberal politician and reformer John Bright. In it, he said: 'England is the mother of Parliaments.'

Mr Balfour's poodle

A derogatory term for the House of Lords in relation to the Prime Minister, which may now sometimes be reworked. The Liberal Democrat peer Lord Goodhart, speaking in the Lords in May 2005 on the government's proposed reform of the House of Lords said:

> Your Lordships' House was described by David Lloyd George in 1907 as, 'Mr Balfour's poodle'. Today it faces a future as 'Mr Blair's chihuahua'; and just in case it should forget itself, the chihuahua is to have its teeth extracted.

The expression looks back to the efforts of the Liberal Government, returned to office on a landslide in 1906, to pass a programme of radical legislation. The Liberal Prime Minister, H. H. Asquith, was supported in his efforts by his Chancellor David Lloyd George: they faced a Conservative Party led by the former Prime Minister Arthur Balfour. Roy Jenkins, writing in 1954 about the resulting conflict between the Asquith Government and the House of Lords, gave his book the title: *Mr. Balfour's poodle: an account of the struggle between the House of Lords and the government of Mr. Asquith*. The book took as its epigraph a comment attributed to David Lloyd George in 1908: 'The House of Lords is not the watchdog of the constitution; it is Mr Balfour's poodle.' However, the earliest 'poodle' reference from Lloyd George in this context comes from the year before, and is worded slightly differently. He said in the House of Commons on 26 June 1907 of the House of Lords: 'The leal and trusty mastiff which is to watch over our interests, but which runs away at the first snarl of the trade unions...A mastiff? It is the right hon. Gentleman's poodle.'

My lips are sealed

In 1935, Italy under Mussolini attacked Abyssinia. The newly-elected British Government, led by Stanley Baldwin as Prime Minister, was aware that there was no public enthusiasm for war, and that military intervention would not be supported by France. The Hoare-Laval Pact, negotiated by the Foreign Ministers for the two countries, allowed the annexation by Italy, although it occasioned widespread criticism.

'My lips are sealed'

'My lips are sealed' are often said to have been Baldwin's words during the Commons debate on the crisis, in December 1935, when he explained that he could not yet divulge the full facts behind the government's actions. What Baldwin actually said was:

> I shall be but a short time tonight. I have seldom spoken with greater regret, for my lips are not yet unsealed. Were these troubles over I would make a case, and I guarantee that not a man would go into the lobby against us.

The *Oxford Dictionary of National Biography* calls the speech 'unconvincing', and notes that the affair damaged confidence in the Prime Minister.

Natural selection is a mechanism for generating an exceedingly high degree of improbability

A well-known summary of the views of the statistician and geneticist R. A. Fisher, which is frequently quoted or alluded to. Richard Dawkins, writing in *Natural History Magazine* in November 2005, said: '**Paraphrasing the twentieth-century population geneticist Ronald Fisher, natural selection is a mechanism for generating improbability on an enormous scale.**'

Fisher's actual words, from an essay 'Retrospect of the criticisms of the Theory of Natural Selection' in Julian Huxley's *Evolution as a Process* (1954), were:

> It was Darwin's chief contribution, not only to Biology but to the whole of natural science, to have brought to light a process by which contingencies a priori improbable are given, in the process of time, an increasing probability, until it is their non-occurrence, rather than their occurrence, which becomes highly improbable.

Nice guys finish last

An alteration of a casual remark at a baseball practice ground by the American coach Leo Durocher. Durocher used the phrase as the title of a book, published in 1975, in which his own account appeared. 'I called off his players' names as they came marching up the step behind him...All nice guys. They'll finish last. Nice guys. Finish last.'

The expression has now become part of the language. A note in the *Guardian* of June 2002 on Robert Altman's 1992 film *The Player* described it as a 'comedy about a ruthless studio executive. Smart satire that proves nice guys finish last in Tinseltown'.

A noble experiment

An article in the *Irish Independent* of June 2001, referring to reports that President Bush's daughters had been trying to buy beer (forbidden in the State of Texas to those under twenty-one) was headed: 'Prohibition is alive and well in Bush's America.' One paragraph of the article began: 'Prohibition is not dead in America. It was ostensibly repealed in 1933 when the Congress passed the 21st Amendment to its Constitution. Herbert Hoover's "Noble Experiment" had failed.'

Prohibition had been enacted in the Eighteenth Amendment to the Constitution, which came into law in 1920, and was in force when Herbert Hoover was elected to the presidency in 1928. In the

February of that year, Hoover had written to Senator William E. Borah, 'Our country has deliberately undertaken a great social and economic experiment, noble in motive and far-reaching in purpose.' He made a similar comment when accepting the Republican nomination in August. The term 'a noble experiment' became the popular summary.

Prohibition was repealed in 1933, during Hoover's second presidency.

Nobody ever lost money by underrating public taste

A wry modern saying referred to by the veteran journalist and columnist W. F. Deedes when he said of Britain's Millennium Dome in 2000: 'The man who said nobody ever lost money by underrating public taste has been proved wrong.'

The saying probably represents a summary of a longer assessment given in the *Chicago Tribune* of September 1926 by the journalist and critic H. L. Mencken:

> No one in this world, so far as I know—and I have searched the records for years, and employed agents to help me—has ever lost money by underestimating the intelligence of the great masses of the plain people.

No plan survives first contact with the enemy

A piece of military wisdom deriving from a formulation by the nineteenth-century Prussian military commander Helmuth von Moltke. He wrote in 1880, 'No plan of operations reaches with any certainty beyond the first encounter with the enemy's main force.'

The warning has been further modified, as in Sean Naylor's article on Operation Anaconda (the hunt for Osama bin Laden) in Afghanistan, published in the *New York Times* of March 2003: 'That the operation didn't go as planned is no disgrace. It is a cliché that no plan survives the first shot fired, but it is no less true for being one.'

Nothing to lose but your yolks

A reworking by the witty American politician Adlai Stevenson, who said in a speech of February 1956, 'Eggheads of the world, arise— I was even going to add that you have nothing to lose but your yolks.'

Stevenson was making a play on the adjuration 'nothing to lose but your yokes', which derives in turn from a passage in *The Communist Manifesto* (1848) by Karl Marx and Friedrich Engels. The original wording runs: 'The proletarians have nothing to lose but their chains. They have a world to win. WORKING MEN OF ALL COUNTRIES, UNITE!'

Not tonight, Josephine

Supposedly said by Napoleon to his wife, the Empress Josephine, but apparently apocryphal; the phrase does not appear in contemporary sources, but was current by the early twentieth century. 'Not tonight, Josephine' was the title of a song (1915), by Worton David and Lawrence Wright, popularized by the music-hall actress Florrie Forde.

'Not tonight Josephine'

The expression is now part of the common vocabulary: a column by Joan Smith in the *Guardian* of September 2000, on why men might refuse sex, was headed, 'Not tonight, Josephine.'

Now Barabbas was a publisher

A well-known (and still quoted) assessment of a publisher as seen from an author's point of view. The original comment was made by the nineteenth-century Scottish poet Thomas Campbell. His authorship of the remark is recorded in Samuel Smiles *A Publisher*

and his Friends: Memoir and Correspondence of the late John Murray.
Describing Campbell's relationship with Murray, Smiles wrote:

> We cannot conclude this account of Campbell's dealing with Murray
> without referring to an often-quoted story which has for many years
> sailed under false colours. It was Thomas Campbell who wrote 'Now
> Barabbas was a publisher', whether in a Bible or otherwise is not
> authentically recorded, and forwarded it to a friend; but Mr Murray was
> not the publisher to whom it referred, nor was Lord Byron, as has been
> so frequently stated, the author of the joke.

Campbell was of course reworking the biblical line in the Authorized
Version's translation of St John's Gospel: **'Now Barabbas was a
robber.'**

O Diamond! Diamond!

According to legend, the reproach **'O Diamond! Diamond!
Thou little knowest the mischief done'** was uttered by the
English mathematician and physicist Sir Isaac Newton when a
pet dog knocked over a candle and set fire to some papers, and
thereby 'destroyed the finished labours of some years'. The story is
recorded in a note to Thomas Maude's *Wensley-Dale...a Poem* (1772),
but is probably apocryphal. There is no reference to a dog in the
recollections of Newton's contemporaries.

The tale of the supposed accident nevertheless became well-
established; Samuel Smiles quotes it in *Self-Help* (1859), in his chapter
on 'Application and Perseverance':

> The accidental destruction of Sir Isaac Newton's papers, by his little
> dog 'Diamond' upsetting a lighted taper upon his desk, by which the
> elaborate calculations of many years were in a moment destroyed, is a
> well-known anecdote, and need not here be repeated: it is said that the
> loss caused the philosopher such profound grief that it seriously injured
> his health, and impaired his understanding.

Old maids bicycling to Holy Communion

In October 1983, addressing the Conservative Group for Europe, the Prime Minister John Major said:

> Fifty years on from now, Britain will still be the country of long shadows on county [cricket] grounds, warm beer, invincible green suburbs, dog lovers, and—as George Orwell said—old maids bicycling to Holy Communion through the morning mist.

John Major had in fact slightly reworded what George Orwell had said in his essay 'England, your England', published in *The Lion and the Unicorn* in 1941: '**Old maids biking to Holy Communion through the mists of the autumn mornings...these are not only fragments, but characteristic fragments, of the English scene.**'

Once aboard the lugger and the maid is mine

A letter in *Notes and Queries* for 31 March 1934 noted that the phrase '**Once aboard the lugger and the girl is mine**' was used in the musical comedy *Floradora* (1899) by Owen Hall and Leslie Stuart. The correspondent added that the saying had been in common use in his boyhood recollection.

The author 'Q' (Sir Arthur Quiller-Couch) took 'Once Aboard the Lugger' as the title of a short story published in the *Tauchnitz Magazine* in March 1892. In this, a young clergyman is decoyed on board her boat by a fisher girl who refuses to return him to shore until he has promised to marry her.

(The phrase 'Once aboard the lugger' is also used by itself. In Kipling's *A Fleet in Being* (1898), the narrator describes his return to the Channel Squadron for a further trip, saying, '**Once aboard the lugger the past twelve months rolled up like a chart that one needs no longer.**')

The origin appears to be a line from *The Gipsy Farmer* (performed 1845) by John Benn Johnstone. In this, a would-be abductor says: '**I**

want you to assist me in forcing her on board the lugger; once there,
I'll frighten her into marriage.'

One indissoluble bond

A number of online sources currently attribute to John Quincy
Adams, sixth President of the United States, the statement that
'The highest glory of the American Revolution is this; it connected
in one indissoluble bond the principles of civil government with the
principles of Christianity.'

It appears, however, that this is not a genuine quotation from
Adams. The earliest citation found for it is in *Pulpit of the Revolution:
or, the political sermons of 1776* (1860) by the American lawyer John
Wingate Thornton (1818–78). Rather than being a quotation directly
attributed to Adams, it seems to be Thornton's summary of what he
believed Adams's views to be.

One small step for man

In July 1969, the American astronaut Neil Armstrong became the
first man on the moon. On landing, he radioed back a prepared
message, which was printed in the *New York Times* of 21 July 1969
in the form 'That's one small step for a man, one giant leap for
mankind.' However, interference in transmission blurred the 'a', and
in a number of reports (including that in the *Times*) the first part of
the message was printed as 'One small step for man'.

The formulation 'one small step...one giant leap' has since become
established in the language, as in the line in a 1997 episode of *The
Simpsons*, 'That's one small step for a kid, one giant leap for kidkind.'

Outside every fat man

In his novel *One Fat Englishman* (1963), Kingsley Amis wrote that
'Outside every fat man there was an even fatter man trying to
close in.' Amis was reworking comments of two earlier writers. Cyril

Connolly had written in *The Unquiet Grave* (1944) that 'Imprisoned in every fat man a thin one is wildly signalling to be let out.' Five years before that, in *Coming up for Air* (1939), George Orwell had written, 'I'm fat, but I'm thin inside. Has it ever struck you that there's a thin man inside every fat man, just as they say there's a statue inside every block of stone?'

The past is not dead

The words 'The past is not dead. It is not even past', attributed to the American writer William Faulkner, form the epigraph for Peter Carey's 2001 novel about the Australian bushranger Ned Kelly, *The True History of the Kelly Gang*. However, what Faulkner actually wrote in his 1951 novel *Requiem for a Nun* differs slightly from this: 'The past is never dead. It is not even past.'

Peace for our time

In September 1938, returning from Munich, the British Prime Minister Neville Chamberlain said in a speech from 10 Downing Street: 'This is the second time in our history that there has come back from Germany to Downing Street peace with honour. I believe it is peace for our time.'

The previous (and more lastingly successful) occasion to which Chamberlain referred had occurred in 1878, when Benjamin Disraeli, Prime Minister at the time, returned from the Congress of Berlin. He said in a speech of 16 July, 'Lord Salisbury and myself have brought you back peace—but a peace I hope with honour.'

The association of 'peace' with 'honour' goes back before Disraeli; in 1853 the British Whig statesman and former Prime Minister, Lord John Russell, declared, 'If peace cannot be maintained with honour, it is no longer peace.' However, another and much earlier antecedent to Chamberlain's comment can be found, in one of the collects for Matins in the *Book of Common Prayer* (1662): 'Give peace in our time, O Lord.'

Pennies don't fall from heaven

In the General Election of May 1979, the Conservatives under Margaret Thatcher defeated the Labour Government of James Callaghan. In November of that year, the new Prime Minister gave her view that, '**Pennies don't fall from heaven. They have to be earned on earth.**'

The reference was to 'Pennies from Heaven' (1936 song) by the American songwriter Johnnie Burke:

> Every time it rains, it rains
> Pennies from heaven.

Play it again, Sam

Supposedly said by Ingrid Bergman, as Isla, in the 1942 film *Casablanca*. However, these exact words do not occur in the screenplay. At one point, Ingrid Bergman says to the pianist, '**Play it, Sam. Play "As Time Goes By".**' (Herman Hupfeld's 1931 song 'As Time Goes By' has been of special significance to Isla and her former lover Rick during their days in Paris.) Later, Humphrey Bogart, as Rick, says: '**If she can stand it, I can. Play it!**'

'Play it again, Sam'

Play the — card

Introduce a specified advantageous, and often political, factor. One of the more notable modern variants was heard, in connection with the O. J. Simpson trial, in 1995. Explaining the defence team's change of strategy, the American lawyer Robert Shapiro said, '**Not only did we play the race card, we played it from the bottom of the deck.**'

The phrase derives from a coinage by the nineteenth-century British Conservative politician, Lord Randolph Churchill. In 1886, the question of Irish Home Rule, favoured by Gladstone's Liberal Government, was one of the hot political topics of the day. Lord

Randolph, a fervent opponent of Home Rule, took the view that the nationalist cause could best be countered by calling on the political majority of Protestant Ulster. He wrote in February to Lord Justice Fitzgibbon:

> I decided some time ago that if the G. O. M. [the 'Grand Old Man, i.e. William Ewart Gladstone] went for Home Rule, the Orange card would be the one to play. Please God it may turn out the ace of trumps and not the two.

Politics is the art of the impossible

In a speech in Prague, 1 January 1990, the Czech dramatist and statesman Václav Havel said:

> Let us teach ourselves and others that politics can be not only the art of the possible, especially if this means the art of speculation, calculation, intrigue, secret deals, and pragmatic manoeuvring, but that it can even be the art of the impossible, namely, the art of improving ourselves and the world.

Havel was reworking an aphorism which had long been part of the political vocabulary. In 1971, the British Conservative politician R. A. Butler wrote in *The Art of the Possible*: '**Politics is the Art of the Possible. That is what these pages show I have tried to achieve—not more—and that is what I have called my book.**' In June 1964, the scientist Peter Medawar gave the phrase a witty twist in the columns of the *New Statesman*: '**If politics is the art of the possible, research is surely the art of the soluble. Both are immensely practical-minded affairs.**' Two years before that, the economist J. K. Galbraith warned President Kennedy in March 1962 that '**Politics is not the art of the possible. It consists in choosing between the disastrous and the unpalatable.**'

This characterization of the essential nature of politics goes back to a statesman of the nineteenth century, the German 'Iron Chancellor', Otto von Bismarck. In August 1867, in conversation with Meyer von Waldeck, he said, '**Politics is the art of the possible.**'

The pound in your pocket

In November 1967, the Labour Government of Harold Wilson
devalued the currency, and Wilson himself made an official
broadcast on the topic. In it he explained:

> From now the pound abroad is worth 14 per cent or so less in terms of
> other currencies. It does not mean, of course, that the pound here in
> Britain, in your pocket or purse or in your bank, has been devalued.

'The pound in your pocket' quickly became a shorthand way of
referring to this broadcast and hence to the devaluation.

Power corrupts

The journalist Andrew Marr wrote in a *Daily Telegraph* column of
October 2004, considering the difficulties of the out-of-office
Conservative Party, '**If power corrupts, and absolute power corrupts
absolutely, then powerlessness presumably makes you purer.**'

Andrew Marr was playing with a dictum of the English historian
Lord Acton which had long been proverbial. Over thirty years before,
in November 1968, a cartoon by Osbert Lancaster was published
in the *Daily Express*. In it a don in mortarboard and gown is seen
confronting two students holding a placard proclaiming 'No Grant.
Cut!' The caption reads: '**May I remind you, gentlemen, of the
words of the great Lord Acton, "All power corrupts, absolute power
corrupts absolutely, but student power can be switched off at the
main."**'

The original statement, to which Marr and Lancaster referred,
appears in a letter of April 1887 from Lord Acton to his friend Bishop
Mandell Creighton. What Acton actually wrote was, '**Power tends to
corrupt and absolute power corrupts absolutely.**'

It is interesting to note that a similar thought had been expressed
even earlier. The poet William Wordsworth, in his tract (published
in 1809) on the Convention of Cintra had written '**There is an
unconquerable tendency in all power...to injure the mind of him who**

exercises that power.' A generation before that, the elder William Pitt, Lord Chatham, speaking in the House of Lords in January 1770, said, 'Unlimited power is apt to corrupt the minds of those who possess it.'

Praise from Sir Hubert is praise indeed

Said to indicate that praise from a particular quarter is well worth having. In Dorothy Sayers' 1935 novel *Gaudy Night*, her amateur detective Lord Peter Wimsey congratulates Harriet Vane on the dossier she has compiled of poison pen attacks at Shrewsbury College:

> At the end of the first few pages he looked up to remark: 'I'll say one thing for the writing of detective fiction: you know how to put your story together; how to arrange the evidence.' 'Thank you,' Harriet said drily, 'praise from Sir Hubert is praise indeed.'

The expression was established by the middle of the nineteenth century, and appears in Charles Dickens' *Dombey and Son* (1848):

> 'Quite so,' assented the Doctor—'and vigorous effort. Mr Pilkins here, who from his position of medical adviser in this family—no one better qualified to fill that position, I am sure.' 'Oh!' murmured the family practitioner. 'Praise from Sir Hubert Stanley!' 'You are good enough,' returned Doctor Parker Peps, 'to say so.'

The origin of the expression is found in *A Cure for the Heartache* (1797), by Thomas Morton. In this play, Young Rapid, radical son of a wealthy tailor, has redeemed his character through loyalty to his sweetheart and assistance to the Stanley family which foils the plans of the malicious Nabob who has designs on Sir Hubert Stanley's estate. His behaviour is applauded by the baronet, bringing the comment, 'Approbation from Sir Hubert Stanley is praise indeed.'

Pray for Shackleton

A saying, reflecting the reputation for competence and effectiveness of the explorer Ernest Shackleton, which implies that when all other hope is gone, there is still a final resort. A fuller version runs, '**When disaster strikes and all hope is gone, get down on your knees and pray for Shackleton.**'

The immediate source for the saying is found in a lecture, 'Twentieth Century Man against Antarctica', given to the British Association for the Advancement of Science in 1950 by the geologist Raymond Priestley. Considering the great names of Antarctic exploration, Priestley said:

> I served both with Shackleton and Scott and very briefly met Amundsen in mid-career. I believe a colleague hit the nail when he wrote: 'As a scientific leader give me Scott; for swift and efficient polar travel Amundsen but when things are hopeless and there seems no way out, get down on your knees and pray for Shackleton.'

Priestley was paraphrasing the explorer Apsley Cherry-Garrard, who had written in *The Worst Journey in the World* (1923):

> For a joint scientific and geographical piece of organization, give me Scott; for a Winter Journey, Wilson; for a dash to the pole and nothing else, Amundsen: and if I am in the devil of a hole and want to get out of it, give me Shackleton every time.

Pride goes before a fall

A column in the *Daily Telegraph* of November 2005, considering the resignation from the Cabinet of David Blunkett, was headed: '**Even in Labour's Britain, pride still goes before a fall.**'

'Pride goes before a fall' which is now a truism, comes ultimately from the Authorized Version's translation of the book of Proverbs: '**Pride goeth before a fall, and a haughty spirit before**

'Pride goes before a fall'

destruction.' The columnist, noting this, went on to suggest that judging by the speeches made in the Commons: '**Labour has modernized this out-of-date proverb. In its version we find: "Pride remains after destruction, and you can feel good about yourself even after you have tripped yourself up".**'

The proper study of mankind is books

In Aldous Huxley's 1921 novel *Crome Yellow*, one of the characters, Mr Wimbush, reflects that 'the pleasures of private reading and contemplation' far outweigh those of 'love and friendship'. Commenting that 'the world...is just becoming literate', he anticipates that the effect of this will be to ensure that more and more people will discover that reading offers 'all the pleasure of social life and none of its intolerable tedium'. Rather than coming together in 'large herds', they will look for 'solitude and quiet'. He concludes, with satisfaction, '**The proper study of mankind is books.**'

The words are a reworking of a line from Pope's *Essay on Man* (1733):

> Know then thyself, presume not God to scan;
> The proper study of mankind is man.

Put me back on my bike

On 13 July 1967, the racing cyclist Tommy Simpson, on the thirteenth stage of the Tour de France, collapsed and died near the summit of Mont Ventoux. (The *Oxford Dictionary of National Biography* notes that although 'dehydration and exhaustion' were initially given as the official cause of his death, it was later recognized that Simpson, in common with other cyclists of the period, had used amphetamines.)

'Put me back on my bike' is popularly quoted as his last words, but according to William Fotheringham's *Put Me Back on My Bike* (2002), what he actually said was '**On, on, on.**'

Rather light a candle than curse the darkness

In January 2006, campaigning in the Canadian General Election, the Conservative leader Stephen Harper said of himself, 'I believe it's better to light one candle than to promise a million light bulbs.'

The idea of the lighting of a single candle as representing significant and valuable individual effort is long established. In 1962, on the death of the humanitarian and former First Lady of the US Eleanor Roosevelt, the American politician Adlai Stevenson said of her: 'She would rather light a candle than curse the darkness, and her glow has warmed the world.'

The saying 'Better to light one candle than to curse the darkness' is the motto of the American Christopher Society (founded 1945), and is said by the Society to derive from 'an ancient Chinese proverb'.

Rearrange the deckchairs on the Titanic

A phrase typifying a pointless attempt to improve features of an irretrievable situation, using the image of the loss of the *Titanic* to signify unavoidable disaster. It represents a summary of a longer statement made by the American Republican politician and presidential adviser Rogers Morton, reported in the *Washington Post* of 16 May 1976.

Morton was campaign manager to Gerald Ford, who as Vice-President had succeeded to the presidency on the resignation of Richard Nixon in 1974. 1976 was the year of the next presidential election. After Ford had lost five out of six primaries to his challenger for the Republican nomination, Ronald Reagan, Morton was asked by a reporter if he would be considering a change of strategy. He replied, 'I'm not going to rearrange the furniture on the deck of the Titanic.'

Rejoice, rejoice

These words, attributed to Margaret Thatcher, are often quoted in a context critical of her. (When in 2002 it was announced that Lady Thatcher would no longer speak publicly, the Labour MP Jackie Ashley wrote in the *Guardian*, '"Rejoice, rejoice"? Oh, yes. The poor, the trade unions and the left are rejoicing as Margaret Thatcher is forcibly retired.')

'Rejoice, rejoice'

In 1998, the BBC showed a profile of Margaret Thatcher's predecessor as Conservative leader, Edward Heath, who to his evident and continuing chagrin had been defeated by her in the Conservative leadership contest of 1979. In the course of the programme, Heath revealed that on hearing of Mrs Thatcher's own fall from power in 1990, he had telephoned his private office with the simple message, '**Rejoice, rejoice, rejoice**'.

Both comments look back to the Falklands War. On 25 April 1982, during the Falklands War, British troops recaptured South Georgia. Margaret Thatcher, speaking to newsman outside Downing Street, told them, '**Just rejoice at that news and congratulate our armed forces and the Marines. Rejoice!**' Subsequently this was more usually quoted as 'Rejoice, rejoice.'

Religion is the foundation of government

A quotation which is now often attributed to the American statesman James Madison, fourth President of the United States. In fact, it derives from a much longer passage, from which individual elements have been extracted, with consequent alteration of syntax and sense. The passage, from 'Memorial and Remonstrance against Religious Assessments' (1785), reads:

> Because finally, 'the equal right of every citizen to the free exercise of his religion according to the dictates of conscience' is held by the same tenure with all our other rights. If we recur to its origin, it is equally the gift of nature; if we weigh its importance, it cannot be less dear to us; if

we consider the 'Declaration of those rights which pertain to the good people of Virginia, as the basis and foundation of government', it is enumerated with equal solemnity, or rather studied emphasis.

Reports of my death have been greatly exaggerated

A phrase which is now part of the language, as in a 2004 column in the *Independent* of December 2004: '**Rumours of the death of panto, it seems, are greatly exaggerated.**' The expression derives from the popular form of a longer statement by the American writer, Mark Twain, which appeared in the *New York Journal* of 2 June 1897: '**The report of my death was an exaggeration.**' The correction was occasioned by newspaper accounts of Twain's being ill or dead. At the time, Twain's cousin James Ross Clemens was seriously ill in London, and it appears that some reports confused him with Samuel Langhorne Clemens (Mark Twain).

The Republic has no need of scientists

The eighteenth-century French scientist Antoine Laurent Lavoisier caused a revolution in chemistry by his description of combustion as the combination of substances with air, or more specifically the gas oxygen. He is regarded as the father of modern chemistry.

In the Terror of 1794, the ruling Jacobin faction of the French Revolution, dominated by Robespierre, ruthlessly executed anyone considered a threat to their regime. Lavoisier, who had earlier been involved with tax reform, was put on trial for tax-farming. According to a popular story, when condemned, he pleaded for more time to complete his scientific work. The apocryphal response '**The Republic has no need of scientists**' is attributed to the presiding judge.

Lavoisier was guillotined on 8 May 1794. The Italian-French astronomer and mathematician Joseph Louis Lagrange commented,

'Only a moment to cut off that head and a hundred years may not give us another like it.'

Responsibility without power

In Tom Stoppard's 1966 play *Lord Malquist and Mr Moon*, the House of Lords is described as representing '**Responsibility without power, the prerogative of the eunuch throughout the ages**'. Stoppard was reworking a phrase, 'power without responsibility', coined by an earlier writer, Rudyard Kipling, in relation to the newspaper proprietor Max Aitken, Lord Beaverbrook. It was later borrowed by Kipling's cousin, Stanley Baldwin.

The details were given in a speech by Earl Baldwin to the Kipling Society in October 1971:

> When [Max] Aitken acquired the *Daily Express* his political views seemed to Kipling to become more and more inconsistent, and one day Kipling asked him what he was really up to. Aitken is supposed to have replied: 'What I want is power. Kiss 'em one day and kick 'em the next'; and so on. 'I see,' said Kipling. 'Power without responsibility: the prerogative of the harlot throughout the ages.' So, many years later, when [Stanley] Baldwin deemed it necessary to deal sharply with such lords of the press, he obtained leave of his cousin [Kipling] to borrow that telling phrase, which he used to some effect on the 18th March, 1931, at...the old Queen's Hall in Langham Place.

In *The Reader* (1995), the Chilean writer Ariel Dorfman gave this another twist: '**Responsibility without power, the fate of the secretary through the ages.**'

Revealed religion has no weight with me

A statement frequently attributed to the eighteenth-century American politician, inventor, and scientist Benjamin Franklin It appears to come from an alteration of a longer passage in Franklin's autobiography:

> Revelation had indeed no weight with me, as such; but I entertain'd an opinion that, though certain actions might not be bad because they were forbidden by it, or good because it commanded them, yet probably these actions might be forbidden because they were bad for us, or commanded because they were beneficial to us, in their own natures, all the circumstances of things considered.

Rivers of blood

A phrase taken to summarize a notorious speech made by the British Conservative politician Enoch Powell in 1968, speaking against the official policy of immigration, and foreseeing a violent outcome. What Powell said, in a speech of April 1968, was, '**As I look ahead, I am filled with foreboding. Like the Roman, I seem to see "the River Tiber foaming with much blood".**' (The reference to 'the Roman' was to the Roman poet Virgil, who in the *Aeneid* had written, '**I see wars, horrible wars, and the Tiber foaming with much blood.**') The speech caused a storm of protest, and Powell was dismissed from the front bench by the Prime Minister, Edward Heath.

'Rivers of blood' in its literal sense was already well-attested, but since Powell's speech it has come to have this specialized reference. In January 2005, the British writer Andrea Levy won the Whitbread Book of the Year Award for her novel *Small Island* (2004), about immigrants from Jamaica in post-War Britain. Accepting the award, she said: '**Most of all I would like to thank all those people in Britain who work hard to make sure the rivers in this country never run with blood, only with water.**'

Rum, sodomy, and the lash

Often quoted, as in Peter Gretton's *Former Naval Person* (1968), as a summing up of the traditions of the Navy by Winston Churchill. However, in the earliest contemporary account, the diary for 17 August 1950 of the diplomat and writer Harold Nicolson, Churchill's wording differs slightly: 'Naval tradition? Monstrous. Nothing but rum, sodomy, prayers, and the lash.'

The Rupert of Debate

In his poem *The New Timon* (1846), the writer and politician Edward Bulwer-Lytton wrote:

> Here Stanley meets,—how Stanley scorns, the glance!
> The brilliant chief, irregularly great,
> Frank, haughty, rash,—the Rupert of Debate!

The subject of these lines was the Conservative politician, and noted orator, Lord Stanley, later Earl of Derby. In likening Stanley to the dashing (but reckless) Cavalier leader Rupert of the Rhine, Bulwer-Lytton was borrowing an image from another Conservative politician, Benjamin Disraeli. Speaking in the House of Commons, 24 April 1844, Disraeli said of Stanley: 'The noble Lord is the Prince Rupert of Parliamentary discussion.'

Safety in numbers

A proverbial formulation, of which the first example is found in Jane Austen's *Emma* (1816). Emma, walking with Harriet, has 'in Emma's opinion, been talking enough of Mr Elton that day'. Accordingly, she plans a diversion. 'They were just approaching the house where lived Mrs and Miss Bates. She determined to call upon them and seek safety in numbers.'

The phrase comes ultimately from the Bible, in the Authorized

Version's translation of the book of Proverbs: 'Where no counsel is, the people fall: but in the multitude of counsellors there is safety.'

Save the gerund, and screw the whale

A witty extension by Tom Stoppard, in his 1982 play *The Real Thing*. The environmental slogan 'Save the Whale' was being used at the time by the campaign to ban commercial whaling in the light of alarm over the rapidly declining whale population. The campaign led to a moratorium on whaling in 1985.

> 'Save the gerund, and screw the whale'

See how these Christians love one another

The usual form in which a longer passage from the early Christian theologian Tertullian is quoted. The eighteenth-century hymn by John and Charles Wesley, 'Giver of Concord, Prince of Peace', has the lines:

> O, let us find the ancient way
> Our wondering foes to move,
> And force the heathen world to say,
> 'See how these Christians love!'

The original passage, from Tertullian's *Apologeticus*, reads in full:

> 'Look,' they say, 'how they [Christians] love one another' (for they themselves hate one another); 'and how they are ready to die for each other' (for they themselves are readier to kill each other).

Selling off the family silver

Parting with a valuable resource for immediate advantage. The phrase is often used in a political context, as in a column from the *Financial Times* of January 2006, headed 'Treasury cashes in on the UK's financial jiggery-pokery'. One paragraph of this column has the comment, 'What we are actually getting very good at is selling off the family silver in ever-increasing quantities, and smoke-and-mirrors financial accounting.'

The phrase is particularly associated with criticism of the privatization policies of Margaret Thatcher, and is often said to have been used by Harold Macmillan in criticizing the trend. What Macmillan had actually said, in a speech to the Tory Reform Group, 8 November 1985, was, 'First of all the Georgian silver goes, and then all that nice furniture that used to be in the saloon. Then the Canalettos go.'

Shaken, not stirred

In February 2004, the *Guardian* published an article by Judith Kneen on the secret services, 'Into the world of the spook'. The first subhead was 'Shaken not stirred', and the following paragraph pointed out that our view of the intelligence services is shaped by what we see and read in films, television dramas, and books.

> It's a glamorous world of fast cars, double-crossing deals and perfect martinis, and that icon of Her Majesty's Secret Service, James Bond, has convinced us that national security is in the safest of hands.

'Shaken, not stirred' is a phrase associated specifically with Ian Fleming's James Bond, and his requirements for making a martini. The precise wording of the instruction can be found in the 1958 thriller *Dr No*: 'A medium Vodka dry Martini—with a slice of lemon peel. Shaken and not stirred.'

Shouting fire in a crowded theatre

Often used as an example of the practical limits of the right to free speech, as in a column on security in the *New York Times* of August 2005. Considering the balance between necessary surveillance and civil liberties, the author of the article, Richard A. Clarke, wrote: 'We must cherish our right to free speech, but just as it is not a right to yell "fire" in a crowded theater, it does not sanction preaching "bomb the subway".'

The expression originally comes from a judgement given by the American lawyer and Supreme Court Justice Oliver Wendell Holmes Jnr. In *Schenck v. United States*, 1919, Justice Holmes wrote:

> The most stringent protection of free speech would not protect a man falsely shouting fire in a theatre and causing a panic...The question on every case is whether the words used are used in such circumstances and are of such a nature as to create a clear and present danger that they will bring about the substantive evils that Congress has a right to prevent.

The sick man of —

A country that is politically or economically unsound, especially in comparison with its neighbours. The term was originally (in the late nineteenth century) applied to the Sultan of Turkey, and later extended to Turkey and other countries. The 'sick man of Europe' was a name for the Ottoman Empire.

The expression derives from a comment by the Russian Emperor Nicholas I in the first part of the nineteenth century: 'Turkey is a dying man. We may endeavour to keep him alive, but we shall not succeed. He will, he must die.' However, a similar thought was expressed early in the eighteenth century by the French political philosopher Montesquieu. Writing in *Lettres Persanes* (1721) on the Ottoman Empire, he said, 'That huge distempered body does not support itself by a mild and temperate regimen; but by violent remedies, which are incessantly corroding and exhausting its strength.'

Sketch the ruins of St Paul's

Lord Macaulay, in *Essays Contributed to the Edinburgh Review* (1843), envisaged a future visitor from New Zealand coming on a ruined London:

She [the Roman Catholic Church] may still exist in undiminished vigour when some traveller from New Zealand shall, in the midst of a vast solitude, take his stand on a broken arch of London Bridge to sketch the ruins of St Paul's.

Macaulay was borrowing a number of images and words from a writer of the preceding century. In November 1775, Horace Walpole wrote to his friend Horace Mann:

The next Augustan age will dawn on the other side of the Atlantic. There will, perhaps, be a Thucydides at Boston, a Xenophon at New York, and, in time, a Virgil at Mexico, and a Newton at Peru. At last, some curious traveller from Lima will visit England and give a description of the ruins of St Paul's, like the editions of Balbec and Palmyra.

Slipped the surly bonds of earth to touch the face of God

In 1986, on the loss of the space shuttle Challenger with all its crew, President Ronald Reagan broadcast from the Oval Office. In one passage, he said:

We will never forget them, nor the last time we saw them this morning, as they prepared for the journey and waved goodbye and 'slipped the surly bonds of earth' to 'touch the face of God'.

In his broadcast, the President was conflating two lines of a poem by the American airman John Gillespie Magee, who was killed in 1941 while flying with the Royal Canadian Airforce. His poem 'High Flight' (1943) opens with the lines:

Oh! I have slipped the surly bonds of earth
And danced the skies on laughter-silver wings.

It closes with the lines:

And, while with silent lifting mind I've trod
The high, untrespassed sanctity of space,
Put out my hand and touched the face of God.

Peggy Noonan, speechwriter for Ronald Reagan, has given an account of writing the text of the broadcast in her 1990 memoir *What I Saw at the Revolution*. She describes her anxiety as to whether the words would be equal to the occasion, and her relief when the broadcast was warmly received. The following month, *Time Magazine* headed its account of the broadcast 'They slipped the surly bonds of earth to touch the face of God.'

Small earthquake in Chile

In January 2003, in a House of Commons debate on the Local Government Bill, the Conservative politician David Curry said:

> We have not really considered whether and how we can reassert representative democracy, so it is not a case of paradise gained or even of nirvana deferred. It is a small earthquake in Walsall, with not many shaken.

'Small earthquake in Chile'

The reference was to a supposed *Times* headline composed by the writer and journalist Claud Cockburn. In his memoir *In Time of Trouble* (1956), Cockburn claimed that, when working at the *Times* in the 1930s, he had won an unofficial competition for the dullest headline to achieve publication: 'Small earthquake in Chile. Not many dead.'

No edition of the *Times* in which this appears has ever been traced, and it seems likely that the 'headline' is apocryphal.

The soft underbelly of Europe

An expression for the part of Occupied Europe which, in the Second World War, was thought to be most vulnerable to Allied invasion. It established itself in the language: D. F. Fleming, writing in 1961 in *The Cold War and its Origins*, said, 'There was no "soft underbelly of Europe"...In Italy it was an exceedingly porcupiny and costly undertaking all the way.'

The phrase, however, is a rewording of the original. Speaking in the House of Commons in November 1942 to announce 'Operation Torch' (the Allied invasion of North Africa as the first step towards Italy and mainland Europe) Churchill said:

> We make this wide encircling movement in the Mediterranean, having for its primary objective the recovery of the command of that vital sea, but also having for its object the exposure of the underbelly of the Axis, especially Italy, to heavy attack.

Some men are born mediocre

In his 1961 novel *Catch-22*, Joseph Heller wrote of his character Major Major that 'Some men are born mediocre, some men achieve mediocrity, and some men have mediocrity thrust upon them.'

Heller was reworking a line from Shakespeare. In *Twelfth Night* (1601), the steward Malvolio is sent a letter by Sir Toby Belch and others to persuade him to pay suit to the Countess Olivia. He is led to believe that Olivia favours him. A passage in the letter urges: 'Be not afraid of greatness: some men are born great, some achieve greatness, and some have greatness thrust upon them.'

Some of the jam we thought was for tomorrow, we've already eaten

A reflection, recorded in 1969, by the Labour politician Tony Benn, when considering the economic benefits to the Labour Government of Harold Wilson to be derived from the resources of oil and gas in the North Sea. (Benn was Minister of Technology from 1966 to 1970; from 1975 to 1979 he would be Secretary of State for Energy.)

The idea of 'never jam today' as the image of a pleasant prospect that never materializes has become generally proverbial. Both usages look back to a much earlier original: the bewildering world of Lewis Carroll's *Through the Looking-Glass* (1872). The White Queen explains

to Alice the terms on which she would employ her as a maid: 'The
rule is, jam tomorrow and jam yesterday—but never jam today.'

Something must be done

In November 1936 the new King, Edward VIII, toured the distressed
areas of south Wales, including the derelict steelworks at Dowlais.
According to the *Western Mail* of 19 November, the day after his visit,
the King said, 'These works brought all these people here. Something
should be done to get them at work again.'

The sentence was reported in varying forms, but the line
'Something must be done' was the one which lodged in the public
mind. Ironically, the visit was shortly afterwards followed by the
King's abdication, on 10 December 1936.

The South is avenged

On 14 April 1865, the American actor John Wilkes Booth, who
had been a passionate supporter of the Confederacy, shot and
killed President Abraham Lincoln. He is said to have exclaimed, '*Sic
semper tyrannis*! ["Thus always to tyrants", the motto of the state
of Virginia] The South is avenged.' However, the second part of
the statement does not appear in any contemporary source, and is
possibly apocryphal.

Speak for England

In Alan Bennett's play *Forty Years On* (1969), the forthcoming
retirement of the long-serving Headmaster of Albion House is to
be marked by a final end-of-term entertainment. Its title, 'Speak for
England, Arthur', looks back to the beginning of the Second World
War, and typifies an evocation of patriotism in a time of need.

A heated debate in the House of Commons, 2 September 1939,
centred on demands that Neville Chamberlain's government should
take a more resolute stand in the wake of Germany's invasion of

Poland. According to popular accounts, the Conservative politician Leo Amery, dissatisfied with Chamberlain's failure to announce an ultimatum to Germany, called out to Arthur Greenwood, the acting Labour Leader, 'Speak for England' (in some versions, '**Speak for England, Arthur**'). The intervention does not appear in Hansard, but Amery himself claimed to have made the appeal, in his memoir *My Political Life* (1955).

The story that he had done so was current at the time. The critic James Agate noted in his diary for 30 October 1939 that he was working at an anthology for the Forces called *Speak for England*. He added '**Clemence Dane gave me the title; it is the phrase shouted in the House the other day when Arthur Greenwood got up to speak on the declaration of war.**' (The novelist Clemence Dane later included a reference to Amery's having made the appeal in her 1955 novel *The Flower Girls*.) However, the diary for 2 September 1939 of the Conservative politician and writer Harold Nicolson gives different wording and a different speaking. According to Nicolson, it was his fellow Conservative Robert Boothby who called out '***You* speak for Britain!**' to Greenwood.

It seems likely, as Nigel Rees has suggested, that Amery's appeal was taken up by others: this would account for the conflict in wording and authorship. It is clear, however, that it is 'Speak for England' that has lodged itself in the language.

Spend less time with one's family

The Labour politician Alan Milburn announced in 2003 that his responsibilities towards a young family meant that he was returning to the back benches. In the spring of 2005, he returned to a wider role to lead Labour's election campaign. The journalist Kevin Maguire commented in a *New Statesman* column of April 2005 that '**Shoulders broader than Alan Milburn's would sag under the weight of criticism since**

'Spend less time with one's family'

he agreed to spend less time with his family to become Labour's election co-ordinator.'

The expression 'spend more time with one's family' is now often used, ironically, of someone (especially a politician) who is seen as putting a good face on a loss of office or position which is in fact regretted. It derives originally from an exchange, in January 1990, between the British Conservative politician Norman Fowler, and the then Prime Minister, Margaret Thatcher. In his formal resignation letter, Fowler wrote: 'I have a young family and for the next few years I should like to devote more time to them.'

In reply, the Prime Minister wrote: 'I am naturally very sorry to see you go, but understand...your wish to be able to spend more time with your family.'

Squeeze Germany till the pips squeak

In the first volume of his history of the Second World War, published in 1948, Winston Churchill later looked back at the decision to impose punitive reparations on a defeated country. In a section headed 'The Follies of the Victors' he wrote:

> The triumphant Allies continued to assert that they would squeeze Germany 'till the pips squeaked'. All this had a potent bearing on the prosperity of the world and the mood of the German race.

Churchill was looking back to a statement made in 1918 by the British politician and businessman Eric Campbell Geddes. A Unionist candidate in the General Election of that year (seen as a 'khaki' election), he was pressed to make clear his position on war reparations to be extracted from Germany. An account of his speech at Cambridge, 10 December 1918, appeared in the *Cambridge Daily News* of the following day. According to this report, Geddes said: 'The Germans, if this Government is returned, are going to pay every penny; they are going to be squeezed as a lemon is squeezed—until the pips squeak.'

A straight sort of guy

News stories in March 2006 about loans to Labour Party funds in relation to names on the honours list provoked a number of op-ed pieces. One of these, a *Guardian* leader commenting on Tony Blair's defence of revelations about party funding, was headed 'A straight sort of guy'. The leader writer, noting the Prime Minister's appeal to the intelligence, understanding, patience, and even mercy of the nation's voters, added, 'It is a tune that has served him well before, effectively a reprise of his 1997 call to be taken on trust as "a pretty straight sort of guy".'

It is the text of the article, rather than the heading, that points to the original wording. In November 1997, in response to criticism of the Government's exemption of Formula One racing from the tobacco advertising ban, Tony Blair was interviewed by John Humphrys on the BBC's *On the Record* programme. In the course of the interview he asserted, 'I am a pretty straight kind of guy.'

Take away these baubles

In July 1997, speaking in the House of Commons against the imposition of a guillotine, the Conservative politician Sir Patrick Cormack said: ' The Government are, indeed, behaving with Cromwellian disdain for this House—one wonders when someone will come in and tell us to "Take away these baubles."'

'Take away these baubles' is the popular version of the words of Oliver Cromwell on dissolving the Rump Parliament in April 1653. According to the account of the parliamentarian Bulstrode Whitelocke, Cromwell ordered: 'Take away that fool's bauble, the mace.' (The mace, which lies on the table in the House of Commons when the Speaker is in the Chair, and the House is therefore in session, is regarded as a symbol of the authority of the House.)

Tectonic plates

A report in the *Guardian* of December 2005 on Charles Kennedy, still at that point Liberal Democrat Leader, noted that Kennedy's New Year message to his party had acknowledged that 'The tectonic plates are moving.'

The current association of tectonic plates with possible changes to party leadership goes back to the previous year, and speculation over the future of Tony Blair as Prime Minister. The journalist Steve Richards, writing in the *Independent* of May 2004, referred to 'Mr Prescott's declaration that the tectonic plates are moving'.

John Prescott's actual words, as reported in the *Times* of 15 May 2004, were, 'When plates appear to be moving, everyone positions themselves for it.'

Tell your kids to get their scooters off my lawn

A robust injunction made in 1996 by the Conservative Chancellor, Kenneth Clarke, to the Party Chairman Brian Mawhinney, in response to comments made on economic matters by political advisers.

The Chancellor was reworking an adjuration by an earlier politician from a rival party, which employed the image of tanks sent in by a repressive Communist regime, rather than the infantile 'scooters'. This was Harold Wilson's 'Get your tanks off my lawn, Hughie', said to have been addressed to the union leader Hugh Scanlon, then President of the Amalgamated Engineering Union. The occasion was supposedly an afternoon in the summer of 1969, when Scanlon and his fellow union leaders Jack Jones (of the Transport and General Workers' Union) and Vic Feather, the TUC General Secretary, were invited to Chequers for tea. According to the *Guardian* obituary of Hugh Scanlon, published in January 2004:

> As Wilson warned of the dangers of any government retreat on their
> trade union legislation plans, Scanlon is said to have been practising his

golf swing. Exasperated by his guest's intractability, the prime minister exploded: 'Get your tanks off my lawn, Hughie.'

(Interestingly, the obituary goes on to note that 'Scanlon later claimed that he had never heard this from Wilson's lips').

That fable of Christ

A phrase attributed to Pope Leo X by anti-Catholic polemic of the sixteenth century. The story is given, for example, in *The Theatre of God's Judgements* (1597) by the virulently anti-Catholic writer and clergyman Thomas Beard. Describing a conversation between Pope Leo ('a Florentine by birth') and Cardinal Bembo ('who also showed himself to bee none of the best Christians in the world, by his Venetian history'), he alleged that the Pope replied, 'That this fable of Christ had brought to him and such as he, no little profit.'

The story is found just over twenty years earlier in *The Pageant of Popes* (1574), a satirical work, by the evangelical polemicist John Bale. Bale wrote:

> For on a time when a Cardinal Bembus did move a question out of the Gospel, the Pope gave him a very contemptuous answer saying: All ages can testify enough how profitable that fable of Christ hath been to us and our company.

Theories pass. The frog remains

In the prologue to Frank Kermode's *An Appetite for Poetry* (1989), he notes having seen pinned to a door in the Life Sciences building at the University of California, the notice: '*Les théories passent. La grenouille reste.*—Jean Rostand.' Kermode comments: 'There is a risk that in the less severe discipline of criticism the result may turn out to be different: the theories will remain but the frog may disappear.'

The reference is to an entry in *Inquiétudes d'un biologiste* (1967) by the French biologist Jean Rostand: '*Le biologiste passe, la grenouille reste*. [The biologist passes, the frog remains.]' The implication of both versions is that the facts on which scientific theories are founded are unchanging, even if particular hypotheses are demolished.

There but for the grace of God go I

The usual form in which words attributed to the sixteenth-century English evangelical preacher and martyr John Bradford are quoted. They appear to derive from a traditional story noted in the article on Bradford (published in 1885) in the first edition of the *Dictionary of National Biography*. The writer, noting that Bradford was of 'singularly gentle character', adds: 'There is a tradition that on seeing some criminals going to execution he exclaimed: "But for the grace of God there goes John Bradford."'

A thing of beauty and a boy forever

In her *A Guide to Men*, published in 1922, the American writer Helen Rowland reflected sardonically that 'Somehow a bachelor never quite gets over the idea that he is a thing of beauty and a boy forever.' Her neat phrase was a reworking of a line from Keats's *Endymion* (1818), 'A thing of beauty is a joy forever.'

A thing of shreds and patches

In Gilbert and Sullivan's *The Mikado* (1885), the Mikado's son Nanki Poo has fled the court to escape an imposed marriage with the elderly Katisha. He takes on the guise of a travelling musician, describing himself in song as:

> A wandering minstrel I—
> A thing of shreds and patches.

With these words, he reworks a contemptuous epithet from Shakespeare's *Hamlet*, applied by

'A thing of shreds and patches'

Hamlet himself to his uncle, the usurper Claudius: 'A king of shreds and patches'.

The thin red line

An archaic term for the British army (relating originally to their red uniforms), which may now appear as a phrase in which the key colour changes to reflect the organization or body concerned. 'Thin blue line' may be used for the police force.

The term derives from an account of the battle of Balaclava, in 1854, by the journalist and war correspondent William Howard Russell. Russell had seen the Russian cavalry charging the British line, and in his book *The British Expedition to the Crimea* (1877) he wrote, '**They dashed on towards that thin red line tipped with steel.**' However, his original dispatch, published in the *Times* of 14 November 1854, had worded the key phrase differently: '**That thin red streak topped with a line of steel**'.

Three bodies no sensible man challenges

The veteran Conservative statesman and former Prime Minister, Harold Macmillan, was reported as saying in February 1981 that: '**There are three bodies no sensible man directly challenges: the Roman Catholic Church, the Brigade of Guards and the National Union of Mineworkers.**' The context was a decision by Margaret Thatcher's Conservative Government to withdraw plans to close twenty-three pits, in the face of threatened national strikes by the NUM. However, Macmillan was presumably recalling advice given by an earlier Conservative Prime Minister, Stanley Baldwin, recorded by Lord Butler in *The Art of Memory* (1982): '**Do not run your nose dead against the Pope or the NUM!**'

Three-fifths of a man

In April 2004 Condoleezza Rice, then United States National Security Advisor, said in an interview, 'When the Founding Fathers said "we the people", they did not mean me. My ancestors were three-fifths of a man.' The phrase was a significant one, and had been used a few years earlier during the American Bicentennial celebrations of 1987. A ceremony at Philadelphia in May 1787 marked the convening of the Constitutional Convention of May 1787. W. Wilson Goode, speaking at the celebrations, said:

> This document did not originally mean all the people. At the convention the states ratified the Constitution including a clause termed The Great Compromise. This compromise counted the more than 700,000 black slaves in our nation not as individuals but only as three-fifths of a man.

Dr Rice and Mayor Goode were both referring directly to the text of the Constitution of the United States, signed in September 1787. The preamble opened, 'We the people of the United States'. Article 1 of the Constitution, setting out its choice of the electorate, continued:

> Representatives and direct taxes shall be apportioned among the several States which may be included within this Union, according to their respective numbers, which shall be determined by adding to the whole number of free persons, including those bound to service for a term of years, and excluding Indians not taxed, three fifths of all other persons.

Throw another shrimp on the barbie

A discussion on the possibility of improving Australian beef sales to Japan was broadcast by the Australian Broadcasting Corporation on 31 October 2002. At the conclusion of the discussion, one participant suggested: 'I wonder if we could recycle Paul Hogan in Japan—throw another cow on the barbie.'

The reference was to a series of commercials made for the Australian Tourist Board in 1984, featuring the actor Paul Hogan. At the conclusion of his address to the audience, extolling the welcome to be found in Australia, he urges them to come 'down under' and promises to 'slip another shrimp on the barbie'. With the alteration of 'slip' to 'throw', the line has become a humorous evocation of Australian hospitality. Its longevity was demonstrated by a report in the *Sydney Morning Herald* of 24 February 2006, on the launch of Tourism Australia's controversial 'So where the bloody hell are you?' campaign. The first paragraph ran: 'We have tried images of the rock, the reef and the bridge. We even threw shrimps on the barbie. Now it seems we have to swear at tourists to get them Down Under.'

The time was out of joint

Lytton Strachey, writing in his satirical *Eminent Victorians* (1918) of the clergyman Hurrell Froude, one of the instigators of the Oxford Movement, that 'The time was out of joint, and he was only too delighted to have been born to set it right.'

'The time was out of joint'

Strachey was borrowing his words from the scene in *Hamlet* in which the troubled Hamlet laments what he sees as an onerous obligation:

> The time is out of joint; O cursèd spite,
> That ever I was born to set it right!

To err is human, but to really foul things up requires a computer

A modern saying, first recorded in the *Farmers' Almanac for 1978*, and often attributed to the American biologist Paul Ehrlich. It offers an extension of a classic original, 'To err is human, to forgive divine', from Alexander Pope's *An Essay on Criticism* (1711). Pope in turn was drawing on earlier sources: the saying 'Humanum est errare [It is human to err]' was known in Latin, and the thought can be found in English back to Chaucer.

To the Puritan all things are impure

The novelist and poet D. H. Lawrence wrote in *Etruscan Places* (1932) that, 'To the Puritan all things are impure, as somebody says.'

His words were a deliberate reworking of a statement, 'To the pure all things are pure', which has had proverbial status since the mid nineteenth century. To take one example, a character in Charles Kingsley's 1850 novel *Alton Locke* describes a visit to Dulwich Picture Gallery in the following terms:

> When I had got half-way up the gallery I looked round for my cousin. He had turned aside to some picture of a Venus which caught my eye also, but which, as I remember now, only raised in me a shudder and a blush...I have learnt to view such things differently now, thank God. I have learnt that to the pure all things are pure.

The saying goes back to the biblical injunction in the book of Titus (in the translation of the Authorized Version), 'Unto the pure all things are pure; but unto them that are defiled and unbelieving nothing is pure.'

Treason is a matter of dates

The journalist Michael White, writing in the *Guardian* of March 2004 on Iain Duncan Smith's fall from the Conservative leadership, commented that 'Treason is famously a matter of dates.' The words are a popular version of the words of the French statesman and cleric Talleyrand, who gave his support alternately to Napoleon and to the Bourbons. Talleyrand was criticized by the Tsar of Russia for having 'betrayed the cause of Europe' by supporting Napoleon. He is supposed to have answered the charge of treason with the words, 'That, Sire, is a matter of dates.'

The triple cord

The Whig politician Edmund Burke, in his *A Letter to a Noble Lord* (1796) referred to 'The king and his faithful subjects, the lords and commons of this realm,—the triple cord, which no man can break.' The image of a 'triple cord' as something unbreakable is an old one, and in this and other uses probably looks back to a verse in the biblical book of Ecclesiastes: '**A threefold cord is not quickly broken.**'

Trip the light fantastic

A humorous formulation meaning 'dance', in particular take part in ballroom dancing. The expression is well established: in a nineteenth-century novel, Mary Jane Holmes's *West Lawn* (1874), a character reflects:

> I used to pity him evenings when I saw him standing over his wife's chair, looking so wistfully at the dancers. She wouldn't let him waltz,—thought it was very improper, and I was told made several remarks not very complimentary to my style of tripping the light fantastic toe.

The expression comes ultimately from Milton's 1645 poem 'L'Allegro', in the injunction to Euphrosyne, one of the Three Graces of Greek mythology:

> Come, and trip it as you go
> On the light fantastic toe.

The truth which makes one free

The American writer Herbert Agar reflected in his book *A Time for Greatness* (1942) that '**The truth which makes men free is for the most part the truth which men prefer not to hear.**' Agar was reworking a biblical verse from St John's Gospel (Authorized Version), '**And ye shall know the truth, and the truth shall make you free.**'

Two wise acres and a cow

A satirical description coined by Noël Coward as a name for the Sitwells, the brothers Osbert and Sacheverell, and their elder sister Edith. (In 1923, Coward parodied the Sitwells' production *Façade* with a scene in his revue *London Calling!* in which the poetess 'Hernia Whittlebot' appeared reciting her poems, accompanied by her brothers 'Gob and Sago Whittlebot'.)

Coward was playing on a political slogan of the nineteenth century, 'three acres and a cow', and associated with the radical politician Jesse Collings and his land reform campaign. The *Oxford Dictionary of National Biography* (2004–) notes that it was Collings who, in 1885, began to use the phrase, which 'for many years was the war-cry of the land-reformers'. It still, in fact, has a proverbial status which has outlasted the memory of Coward's jibe. In a House of Commons debate of 12 July 2001, the Conservative politician David Curry said that '**Organic farming has moved out of the "three acres and a cow" period of its development.**'

Up like a rocket, down like a stick

An evocation of notable but fleeting success, which has become proverbial. In a *Daily Telegraph* article of May 2000 on the stock market, the saying 'up like a rocket, down like a stick' is referred to as 'a stock market adage'.

The use of the image appears to go back to the words of the radical Tom Paine, in his *Letter to the Addressers on the Late Proclamation* (1792). Paine was responding specifically to what he termed 'Mr Burke's rude and outrageous attack on the French Revolution': that is, Edmund Burke's *Reflections on the Revolution in France*, published in 1790.

The article on Burke in the *Oxford Dictionary of National Biography* notes that Burke's political friends and allies had been dismayed by the extravagance of his language in the *Reflections*. His friend Philip Francis, to whom a draft had been shown, is quoted as saying,

'The mischief you are going to do yourself is, to my apprehension, palpable.' He presumably foresaw something like the criticism to be levelled by Tom Paine. Most famously, in *The Rights of Man* (1791), Paine commented that '**He pities the plumage, but forgets the dying bird.**' The following year, in his *Letter to the Addressers*, he used the rocket image to describe the effect on Burke's reputation:

> To overthrow Mr Burke's fallacious book was scarcely the operation of a day. Even the phalanx of placemen and pensioners, who had given the tone to the multitude, by clamouring forth his political fame, became suddenly silent; and the final event to himself has been, that as he rose like a rocket, he fell like the stick.

Variety is the spice of life

A modern proverb which in this form derives from a line from Cowper's poem *The Task* (1785):

> Variety's the very spice of life,
> That gives it all its flavour.

The idea behind the saying, however, can be traced back much earlier, to the fifth century BC. The Greek dramatist Euripides wrote in the play *Orestes*, '**A change is nice**'.

The voice we heard was that of Mr Churchill

In the General Election campaign of 1945, Winston Churchill's opening broadcast warned against the probable totalitarian approach of a Labour Government by prophesying that they would introduce 'some kind of Gestapo, no doubt humanely administered in the first instance'. This linking of Labour with the methods of Nazi Germany caused a good deal of offence, but the Labour leader Clement Attlee commented dryly: '**The voice we heard was that of Mr Churchill, but the mind was that of Lord Beaverbrook.**'

Attlee was making a biblical allusion. In the story, in the book of Genesis, of how Jacob tricked their father Isaac into blessing him rather than his brother Esau, the deluded father, realizing too late what has happened, exclaims: 'The voice is Jacob's voice, but the hands are the hands of Esau.'

Vox populi, vox humbug

The Union General William Tecumseh Sherman, writing to his wife in June 1863, said in his letter, 'Vox populi, vox humbug.' He was referring to the proverbial '*Vox populi, vox Dei* [The voice of the people is the voice of God]' which has been traced back to the writings of the eighth-century English scholar and theologian Alcuin:

> *Nec audiendi qui solent dicere, Vox populi, vox Dei, quum tumultuositas vulgi semper insaniae proxima sit.* [And those people should not be listened to who keep saying the voice of the people is the voice of God, since the riotousness of the crowd is always very close to madness.]

Hugh Rawson and Margaret Miner, in their 2005 *Oxford Dictionary of American Quotations*, point out a similar scepticism in the eighteenth-century American politician Alexander Hamilton: 'The voice of the people has been said to be the voice of God...It is not true in fact. The people are turbulent and changing; they seldom judge or determine right.'

War is the continuation of politics by other means

A simplification of the words of the nineteenth-century Prussian soldier and military theorist Karl von Clausewitz. The expression is well enough known to be used allusively: a *Guardian* article on the forthcoming Athens Olympics, in August 2004, noted that:

> After the cold war ended, there were high hopes that the Olympic movement would be able to revive its ideals for a new age. For three decades international sport had been the continuation of politics by

other means, with boycotts, counter-boycotts and an obsessive totting up of 'free world' versus 'socialist bloc' medals.

What Clausewitz actually wrote (in *On War*, 1832–4) was a little less absolute: 'War is nothing but a continuation of politics with the admixture of other means.'

A similar thought was expressed by Mao Zedong in 1938: 'Politics is war without bloodshed while war is politics with bloodshed.'

The war to end war

A phrase applied particularly to the First World War, and associated with the writer H. G. Wells, who in 1914 set out the case for supporting the Allied cause in his book *The War that will end War*, and with President Woodrow Wilson. However, the first use of the actual phrase is found in George Bernard Shaw's 1921 play *Back to Methuselah*: 'There was a war called the War to End War. In the war which followed it about ten years later, none of the soldiers were killed, but seven of the capital cities of Europe were wiped out of existence.'

Warts and all

With no attempt to conceal blemishes, inadequacies, or unattractive qualities. The expression occurs in Somerset Maugham's 1930 novel, *Cakes and Ale*, in the question 'Don't you think it would be more interesting if you went the whole hog and drew him warts and all?' It is found earlier, with a more direct reference to its original, in Frederick William Thomas's account of notable nineteenth-century American politician, *John Randolph, of Roanoke, and Other Sketches of Character* (1853). Considering statuary of major political figures, Thomas wrote:

> We saw in the Patent Office the very clothes that General Washington wore, and we look at the statue and at once feel how unlike him it looks. Fancy General Washington sitting to a Daguerreotypist and arraying

himself in a Roman toga for the occasion. A statue should be as much as possible a Daguerreotype of the man.

'Paint me as I am—warts and all,' said Cromwell to the artist, 'or I will not pay you for the picture.' The bluff and bold Protector showed what was the artist's duty in this remark.

The words 'warts and all' are a popular summary of Oliver Cromwell's instructions to the court painter Peter Lely, as recorded in Horace Walpole's *Anecdotes of Painting in England* (1763):

> Mr Lely, I desire you would use all your skill to paint my picture truly like me, and not flatter me at all; but remark all these roughnesses, pimples, warts, and everything as you see me; otherwise I will never pay a farthing for it.'

Was für plundern!

German for 'What a place to plunder!' This was supposedly said, of London, by the Prussian field-marshal Gebhard von Blücher, when surveying the city from the Monument in June 1814. What he actually said was, '*Was für Plunder!* [What rubbish!].'

The story was recounted in some detail by a direct descendant, as recorded in Princess Blücher's *Memoirs of Prince Blücher*, published in 1932:

> While he [Marshal Blücher] was being shown the sights, he climbed the Monument and looked over London from its top. An Englishman accompanying him was expatiating on the magnificence of the vista when Blücher the outspoken, who could hardly see the muddy Thames a few dozen yards away, impatiently muttered '*Was für plunder*', the literal translation of which is 'What rubbish', and referred to the Englishman's vapourings about the roofs, smoke and fog which were all that were visible.

The younger Blücher then highlighted neatly the familiar process of development of a misquotation: '**People standing by partly overheard the remark and, as people will about famous persons, distorted it** into a statement that Blücher had said 'What a place to plunder': thus is history so often made.'

Watch what we do, not what we say

Writing in the *Washington Post* of June 2004, the journalist Richard Cohen said:

> The apparent policy of the Bush administration is to keep combat deaths to a minimum—even if that means letting the bad guys go. It has enacted the doctrine first enunciated by Richard Nixon's attorney general, John Mitchell, who, in paraphrase, said, 'Watch what we do and not what we say.

The reference was to a meeting that took place in July 1969, when John Mitchell, then US Attorney-General, met civil rights workers who were protesting against the policies of the Nixon Administration. According to Suzy Platt's *Respectfully Quoted* (1989), he was heard to say that 'You will be better advised to watch what we do instead of what we say.'

We are the masters now

After the Labour landslide of May 1997, the new Prime Minister warned his MPs: 'We are not the masters. The people are the masters. We are the servants of the people...What the electorate gives, the electorate can take away.' Tony Blair was referring to a notorious assertion made by an earlier Labour politician, Hartley Shawcross, Attorney-General in the Attlee Government. In April 1946, a bill on trade union legislation was undergoing its third reading. To make his point, Shawcross drew on words from Lewis Carroll's *Through the Looking-Glass* (1872), and went on to add his own comment:

'We are the masters now'

> 'But,' said Alice, 'the question is whether you can make a word mean different things.' 'Not so,' said Humpty-Dumpty, 'the question is which

is to be the master. That's all.' We are the masters at the moment, but for
a very long time to come.'

Condensed to 'We are the masters now', the assertion was long
remembered. According to the *Guardian*'s obituary of Lord
Shawcross, he himself once described it as 'the most stupid thing
I've ever said'.

A week is a long time in politics

Attributed to Harold Wilson, and probably first said at a lobby
briefing for journalists at the time of the sterling crisis in 1964.
Interestingly, as Nigel Rees in *Brewer's Quotations* (1994) records,
Wilson himself, when asked just after his retirement as Prime
Minister in 1977, could not pinpoint the precise occasion on which
he first used the words.

It has now achieved the status of a political saying, and it may well
be that Wilson himself was unconsciously drawing on traditional
political wisdom. The Liberal politician Joseph Chamberlain is
recorded in 1886 as having said '**In politics, there is no use in looking
beyond the next fortnight.**'

A wee pretendy Parliament

A dismissive summary of what was at the time the projected
Scottish Parliament, attributed to the Scottish comedian
Billy Connolly. The phrase is a shorter version of what Connolly
actually said when interviewed on *Breakfast with Frost*, in February
1997. Summing up his attitude to the proposals for devolution
(implemented later in the year after Labour came into office),
he said, '**I don't want a Stormont. I don't want a wee pretendy
government in Edinburgh.**'

We have met the enemy, and he is us

A caption to a 1970s cartoon by the American cartoonist Walt Kelly. In it, the cartoon-strip character Pogo the opossum is looking at litter under a tree (the cartoon was subsequently used as an Earth Day poster in 1971).

The declaration is an echo of a much earlier original. On 10 September 1813, Oliver Hazard Perry sent a message to General William Henry Harrison reporting the British surrender at the Battle of Lake Erie. The message ran, '**We have met the enemy and they are ours; two ships, two brigs, once schooner, and one sloop.**'

We must educate our masters

A popular summary of a speech made in July 1867 on the passing of the Reform Bill by the British Liberal politician Robert Lowe, later Lord Sherbrooke. An example of this form is found in G. K. Chesterton's 1917 *The Utopia of Usurers and other Essays*:

> The modern barons...can sign their own names, and that is about all they can do. They cannot face a fact, or follow an argument, or feel a tradition; but, least of all, can they, upon any persuasion, read through a plain impartial book, English or foreign, that is not specially written to soothe their panic or please their pride. Looking up at these seats of the mighty I can only say, with something of despair, what Robert Lowe said of the enfranchised workmen: 'We must educate our masters.'

While this condensed version is clearly in the spirit of what Lowe thought, his actual words differed slightly. He said, '**I believe it will be absolutely necessary that you should prevail on our future masters to learn their letters.**'

We trained hard . . .

In full, 'We trained hard . . . but it seemed that every time we
were beginning to form up into teams we would be reorganized
I was to learn later in life that we tend to meet any new situation
by reorganizing; and a wonderful method it can be for creating the
illusion of progress while producing confusion, inefficiency, and
demoralization.' A saying, recorded from the late twentieth century,
which is frequently attributed to the Roman satirist Petronius
Arbiter, but for which no classical evidence has been found to exist.

What a glorious morning for America

Traditionally quoted form of an exclamation by the American
revolutionary leader Samuel Adams, on hearing the gunfire
at Lexington, 19 April 1775. The words in this form are now on the
town seal of Lexington. A variant form of words is, '**What a glorious
morning is this.**'

The two versions may be blended, as in Benson J. Lossing's *Our
Country* (1875–8), a 'household history' of the United States:

> The bells that were rung on that warm April morning...tolled the knell of
> British domination in the old thirteen colonies. When the firing began,
> Samuel Adams was lingering in his tardy flight on a wooded hill near
> Clarke's house, and when the air was rent by the first volley on Lexington
> Common, he uttered these remarkable words: 'What a glorious morning
> for America is this!' With the vision of an inspired seer at that moment,
> the sturdy patriot perceived in the future the realization of this cherished
> dreams of independence for his beloved country. Those words are
> inscribed on the Lexington Centennial Medal.

What are you going to do about it?

Supposedly the challenge of 'Boss' Tweed to those protesting at the political corruption of New York under the control of Tammany Hall and the Tweed Ring. The words actually derive from a caption to one of Thomas Nast's cartoons.

The German-born cartoonist's work was ultimately highly damaging to Tweed's Tammany domination of New York. The cartoon 'Under the Thumb', published in *Harper's Weekly* of June 1871, showed a giant hand, with Tweed's name on the cufflink, putting its thumb down over Manhattan. The caption ran: '**The Boss. "Well, what are you going to do about it?"**' The key question 'What are you going to do about it?' was also attached to a later cartoon, of November 1871, which depicted 'The Tammany Tiger loose'.

Whatever 'in love' means

Popular version of the reply given by the Prince of Wales in an interview of February 1981, on the announcement of his engagement to Lady Diana Spencer.

'Whatever "in love" means' The words form the first line of a poem, 'September, 1997', written by Carol Ann Duffy on the death of Diana, Princess of Wales. They also featured some years later in news reports of tapes made by the Princess, in which she is heard saying about the interview, 'And Charles turned around and said, "whatever in love means".'

In the course of the interview, the Prince was asked if he was 'in love'. He replied: '**Yes...whatever that may mean.**'

What the soldier said isn't evidence

A mid-nineteenth-century summary of the bar to the admission of hearsay evidence, which is set out at greater length in Charles Dickens's *The Pickwick Papers* (1837):

> 'Little to do, and plenty to get, I suppose?' said Sergeant Buzfuz, with jocularity. 'Oh, quite enough to get, sir, as the soldier said ven they ordered him three hundred and fifty lashes,' replied Sam. 'You must not tell us what the soldier, or any other man, said, sir,' interposed the judge; 'it's not evidence.'

Whenever I hear the word culture, I reach for my pistol

One of the 'Sayings of the Year' recorded in the *Observer* for January 1961 was the remark **'When politicians and civil servants hear the word "culture" they feel for their blue pencil.'** Attributed to Lord Esher, it was the reworking of a comment often attributed to the Nazi leader Hermann Goering, **'Whenever I hear the word culture, I reach for my pistol.'**

The origin of both lines is found in the 1933 play *Schlageter* by the German dramatist Hanns Johst. In the play, a character says, *'Wenn ich Kultur höre...entsichere ich meinen Browning!* [Whenever I hear the word culture...I release the safety-catch of my Browning!]' *Schlageter* was a nationalistic play based on the life of Albert Leo Schlageter, who was court-martialled by the French and shot in 1923 for taking part in active resistance to French occupation of the Ruhr. It was popular with the National Socialist regime, which may help to explain the attribution to Goering.

When Greek meets Greek, then comes the tug of war

A proverbial assertion which is now so well-known that it may be used allusively, as in Aldous Huxley's *Two or Three Graces* (1926): 'When Greek meets Greek then comes, in this case, an exchange of anecdotes about the deposed sovereigns of eastern Europe—in a word, the tug of bores.' An 1804 entry in the *Journals and Notebooks* of the American writer Washington Irving provides an earlier, and also humorous, use: 'Two upright postilions...were disputing who was the greatest rogue..."When Greek meets Greek then comes the tug of war."'

The saying derives originally from a play by the seventeenth-century dramatist Nathaniel Lee. In *The Rival Queens, or the Death of Alexander the Great*, the veteran soldier Clytus is shocked by the favour shown to the Persians. He compares Alexander unfavourably with Philip of Macedon:

> Your father Philip—I have seen him march,
> And fought beneath his dreadful banner, where
> The stoutest at this table would have trembled.
> Nay frown not, Sir, you cannot look me dead.
> When Greeks joined Greeks, then was the tug of war,
> The laboured battle sweat, and conquest bled.

When he cried the little children died in the streets

The concluding words of W. H. Auden's 1940 poem 'Epitaph on a Tyrant'. Auden was reworking a famous passage from *The Rise of the Dutch Republic* (1856) by the American historian John Lothrop Motley. Motley was writing of the Protestant hero William of Orange ('William the Silent'), who in the sixteenth century emerged the key figure to oppose Spanish rule in the Netherlands, and who is regarded as the founding father of the United Provinces of the Netherlands. He was assassinated in 1584. Motley wrote of him: 'As long as he lived, he was the guiding-star of a whole brave nation, and when he died the little children cried in the streets.'

When in Rome, do as the Romans do

Proverbial advice, recorded in this form from the late fifteenth century. It derives ultimately from a saying of St Ambrose, recorded in the *Letters* of St Augustine: 'When I go to Rome, I fast on Saturday, but here [in Milan] I do not. Do you also follow the custom of whatever church you attend, if you do not want to give or receive scandal.'

When it's steam engine time, people invent steam engines

This statement, and the phrase 'steam engine time', is often attributed to the American journalist and student of paranormal phenomena, Charles Hoy Fort. Brooks Landon, in his *Science Fiction after 1900* (2002), noted that it appeared in Harlan Ellison's *Dangerous Visions* (1967), an early and important anthology of science fiction:

> Employing a phrase that would again become a rallying cry for cyberpunk writers some 20 years later, Ellison cited Charles Fort's theory about 'steam engine time'—when it's time for the steam engine to be invented, it will be invented.

Fort's concept of the moment developing for 'steam-engine time' was originally developed in a longer passage of his 1931 book *Lo!*:

> If human thought is a growth, like all other growths, its logic is without foundation of its own, and is only the adjusting constructiveness of all other growing things. A tree cannot find out, as it were, how to blossom,

until comes blossom-time. A social growth cannot find out the use of
steam engines, until comes steam-engine time.

When the legend becomes fact, print the legend

A line from the 1962 film *The Man Who Shot Liberty Valance*, written
by Willis Goldbeck and James Warner Bellah. In the film, the
young lawyer Ransom Stoddard, played by James Stewart, with the
help of the cowboy Tom Doniphon (John Wayne) confronts the
notorious outlaw Liberty Valance (Lee Marvin). Stoddard wants
to defeat Valance using the law, but the outlaw is ultimately shot
by Doniphon—although credit for the shooting is given publicly
to Stoddard. Known, by means of the printed legend, as 'the man
who shot Liberty Valance', he will go on to become a United States
Senator, while Doniphon lives and dies in obscurity.

The film line was a reworking of the words from the original short
story (of 1953) by Dorothy Johnson: '**If the myth gets bigger than the
man, print the myth.**'

Where every prospect pleases

A formula which (especially as followed by the qualification 'and
only man is vile') is often now used to indicate a particularly
beautiful (and unspoilt) place. The expression is an established
one: in his 1911 memoir *A Bishop amongst Bananas*, Herbert Bury, the
former Bishop of British Honduras and Central America, wrote: '**It is
really a country "where every prospect pleases and only man is vile",
for Guatemala is abominably governed and terribly oppressed.**'

The phrase is taken from Reginald Heber's 1821 hymn 'From
Greenland's Icy Mountains'. There is however one key difference,
which has allowed the phrase to be used as a description without
further qualification. Heber's original lines ran:

Though every prospect pleases,
And only man is vile.

He was not primarily directing attention to a place of natural beauty, but suggesting that even with these advantages, something (the recognition of God) is still lacking.

Where's the beef?

Often attributed to the American Democratic politician Walter Mondale. In a televised debate with fellow Democrat Gary Hart, campaigning for the 1984 presidential nomination, Mondale challenged his opponent: **'When I hear your new ideas I'm reminded of that ad, "Where's the beef?"** The allusion was to a slogan for Wendy's Hamburgers, launched in that year. In it, an elderly lady played by the actress Clara Peller, looking at the large bun and small hamburger supposedly produced by a competitor, demanded angrily, 'Where's the beef?'

'Where's the beef?'

While there is death there is hope

A cynical comment attributed to the British Labour politician Richard Crossman, on the death of the Labour leader Hugh Gaitskell in 1963. (According to Crossman himself, it was a favourite remark of the Labour politician Harold Laski.) The line reworks the proverbial **'While there's life there's hope'**: a saying recorded in English from the mid sixteenth century, but with origins going back to classical times.

A white glove pulpit

A phrase coined by Nancy Reagan, who as wife of Ronald Reagan was First Lady of the United States from 1981 to 1989. Mrs Reagan said, in an interview of March 1988, **'If the President has a bully pulpit, then the First Lady has a white glove pulpit...more refined, restricted, ceremonial, but it's a pulpit all the same.'**

In reworking the phrase 'bully pulpit', Nancy Reagan was referring to the words of an earlier Republican president. 'Bully' was a favourite adjective of Theodore Roosevelt, and in 1909, giving his personal view of the presidency, he exclaimed triumphantly, 'I have got such a bully pulpit!'

The white heat of technology

The phrase 'white heat of technology' is often said to have been coined by the British Labour Prime Minister Harold Wilson. A column in the *New York Times* of April 1996 suggested that in the 1960s, John F. Kennedy's 'New Frontier' could be seen to 'find an echo in Harold Wilson's 1964 campaign pledge to forge a new prosperous era through the "white heat of technology".'

'White heat of technology' is actually a paraphrase of what Wilson said, in a speech to the Labour Party Conference of 1963, the year before Labour won the General Election. What he actually said was: 'The Britain that is going to be forged in the white heat of this revolution will be no place for restrictive practices or for outdated methods on either side of industry.'

Who breaks a butterfly on a wheel?

In June 1967, defending the rock star Mick Jagger after his arrest for possessing cannabis, a leader in the *Times* demanded, 'Who breaks a butterfly on a wheel?'

The image of the butterfly broken on the wheel to suggest the destruction of something fragile by unnecessary force is long established. A character in Winifred Holtby's 1931 novel *Poor Caroline* says, 'I can't bear to see a woman in the dock—butterfly on the wheel.' In Trollope's *The Way We Live Now* (1874), the publishers Mr Alf and Mr Booker are discussing the crushing review given to Lady Carbury's *Criminal Queens*. They agree that it is 'a bad book, a thoroughly rotten book', but Mr Alf then says: 'I should have said that violent censure or violent praise would be equally thrown

away upon it. One doesn't want to break a butterfly on the wheel;—
especially a friendly butterfly.'

The expression was even used allusively: when in 1884 Henry
Arthur Jones and Henry Herman collaborated on a version of Ibsen's
A Doll's House in which Nora repents and returns to her family, it was
called *Breaking a Butterfly*.

The original source of the image is Pope's poem 'An Epistle to Dr
Arbuthnot' (1735). In lines attacking (and dismissing) Lord Hervey,
under the name of 'Sporus', Pope wrote:

Satire or sense, alas! can Sporus feel?
Who breaks a butterfly upon a wheel?

In this couplet, the fragility of the subject is seen as part of his
contemptible weakness.

Whom the gods wish to destroy they first call promising

A judgement by the English writer Cyril Connolly in his *Enemies
of Promise* (1938). The allusion is to the proverb '**Whom the gods
would destroy, they first make mad.**' This is first recorded in English
in this form in the late nineteenth century, but the thought goes
back much further. In Ben Jonson's play *Catiline* (1611), Cicero says:

It is a madness
Wherewith heaven blinds them, when it would confound them.

Ultimately the saying goes back to classical origins.

Whose woods these are everybody knows exactly

The humorous writer P. J. O'Rourke, using these words to evoke
a New England community in the 1990s, goes on to point
out further areas of knowledge: who got the woods rezoned for
development as a shopping mall, who failed to get the necessary
financing for the project, and why.

The key introductory words are a reworking of a famous line from American poetry. The opening line of Robert Frost's 1923 poem, 'Stopping by Woods on a Snowy Evening', runs: '**Whose woods these are I think I know.**'

Why don't you come up and see me sometime?

The critic Philip French's review of a biography of the actress Mae West, published in the *Observer* of October 2005, was headed 'Come up and see her'. The reference, instantly recognizable, was to the popular alteration of the invitation uttered by Mae West in the 1933 film *She Done Him Wrong*.

In the film, the actual words of 'Diamond Lil', played by West, are, '**Why don't you come up some time, and see me.**'

Why is this lying bastard lying to me?

Frequently alluded to as a question which the journalist and broadcaster Jeremy Paxman asks himself when embarking on an interview. However, although Paxman is said once to have quoted the statement, he did not originate it. It comes from the memoirs of an earlier journalist, Louis Heren.

In his memoir *Growing Up on The Times* (1978), Heren described how, as a general reporter, he was hurriedly assigned to do the work of an industrial correspondent and cover the fuel crisis of 1946–7. Officials of the Ministry of Labour (possibly also reacting badly to what Heren called his 'natural scepticism') refused to give him the official handouts. He was able to gain access to these only through the helpfulness of a colleague, the industrial correspondent of the *Daily Worker*. Noting that the *Times* readers were thus indebted to the good offices of a communist for the official line, he added:

> The *Worker* man was also a mentor of sorts. One day, when I asked him for some advice before interviewing the permanent secretary, he said,

'Always ask yourself why these lying bastards are lying to you.' I still ask
myself that question today.

Will it play in Peoria?

A catchphrase, meaning 'Will it be acceptable to middle America?',
which was strongly associated with the
administration of Richard Nixon in the early 1970s.
William Safire, in Safire's *New Political Dictionary*
(1993), quoted Nixon's presidential aide John
Ehrlichman as saying that he first used the phrase
to trainee political workers in 1968. Ehrlichman
added:

> Onomatopoeia was the only reason for Peoria, I suppose. And it
> personified—exemplified—a place, removed from media centers on
> the coasts, where the national verdict is cast, according to the Nixon
> doctrine.

The *American National Biography* entry for the nineteenth-century
lawyer and orator Robert Ingersoll recounts an anecdote suggesting
a similar, but much earlier, use of Peoria's name. In 1866, President
Andrew Johnson was in disagreement with the Radical Republican
Congress over the policy of Reconstruction in the Southern States,
going so far as to veto a civil rights bill. When he was asked by a
journalist (from the London *Times*) about the opposition he was
encountering, the President is said to have shown him a telegram
of support from Peoria, saying 'Look at Peoria' (as typifying
heartland support). Ingersoll and his brother Clark, a member of
Congress, were opposed to the President's policies. When Clark
was successfully re-elected to Congress, the Radical Republicans
celebrated with the words '**Now look at Peoria.**'

Winning isn't everything, it's the only thing

An assertion widely associated with the American footballer and coach Vince Lombardi. The attribution has been disputed, as recounted in detail by Hugh Rawson and Margaret Miner in the *Oxford Dictionary of American Quotations* (2005). The quotation has also been credited to the coach Henry 'Red' Sanders (1905–58). Lombardi himself suggested that his own wording had been less aggressive, along the lines of 'Winning isn't everything, but wanting (or making the effort) to win is.'

Winter of discontent

A period of difficulty, especially involving political or industrial unrest; it is specifically used for the winter of 1978–9 in Britain, when widespread strikes finally led to the downfall of the government. The phrase is now established enough for the season to be varied: a report on the BBC News website for 8 July 2002, reporting a vote for strike action by council workers across England, Wales, and Northern Ireland, was headed 'Summer of discontent'.

This particular usage goes back to an interview of February 1979, given by the Labour Prime Minister James Callaghan. He said, 'I had known it was going to be a "winter of discontent".' His government finally lost a vote of no confidence in the House of Commons in March of that year, and was defeated in the subsequent General Election. In the run-up to the election, the *Sun* newspaper used 'Winter of discontent' as a headline.

The origin of the phrase is much earlier, and more literary: the opening line spoken by Richard of Gloucester in Shakespeare's play *Richard II* (1591):

Now is the winter of our discontent
Made glorious summer by this sun of York.

Yes, wonderful things

In November 1922, the tomb of Tutankhamun was discovered in Egypt's Valley of the Kings by the archaeologist Howard Carter, and his patron Lord Carnarvon: the excavation was carried out through the following months. 'Yes, wonderful things' is popularly quoted as the reply given by Carter, when he was asked if he could see anything when first looking into the tomb. However, his notebook records the words as, '**Yes, it is wonderful**.'

In the key passage of the later account (in *The Tomb of Tut.ankh. amen*, 1933), Carter began by describing the overall impression of the room:

> Details of the room within emerged slowly from the mist, strange animals, statues, and gold—everywhere the glint of gold. For the moment—an eternity it must have seemed to the others standing by—I was struck dumb with amazement, and when Lord Carnarvon inquired anxiously 'Can you see anything?' it was all I could do to get out the words, 'Yes, wonderful things!'

The account in Carter's notebook for 26 November 1922, while no less factually dramatic, makes less use of literary effect:

> The interior of the chamber gradually loomed...with its strange and wonderful medley of extraordinary and beautiful objects. Lord Carnarvon said to me 'Can you see anything?' I replied to him, 'Yes, it is wonderful.'

H. V. Winstone, in his *Howard Carter and the Discovery of the Tomb of Tutankhamun* (1991) commented that 'The later version of the finding of the tomb portrays Carter's ability to reconstruct the event in prose of astonishing and perfect harmony.'

You cannot strengthen the weak by weakening the strong

Attributed to Abraham Lincoln by Ronald Reagan. In his speech to the Republican National Convention of 1992, Reagan quoted Lincoln as saying:

> You cannot strengthen the weak by weakening the strong. You cannot help the wage-earner by pulling down the wage-payer. You cannot help the poor by destroying the rich. You cannot help men permanently by doing for them what they could and should do for themselves.

Suzy Platt in *Respectfully Quoted* (1989) gave a frequently-quoted list which is clearly the source for this:

> 1. You cannot bring about prosperity by discouraging thrift. 2. You cannot strengthen the weak by weakening the strong. 3. You cannot help small men up by tearing big men down. 4. You cannot help the poor by destroying the rich. 5. You cannot lift the wage-earner by pulling the wage-payer down. 6. You cannot keep out of trouble by spending more than your income. 7. You cannot further the brotherhood of man by inciting class hatred. 8. You cannot establish sound social security on borrowed money. 9. You cannot build character and courage by taking away a man's initiative and independence. 10. You cannot help men permanently by doing for them what they could and should do for themselves.

She went on to point out that while since the 1940s these 'Ten Points' as attributed to Lincoln have been widely reprinted, there is no reason to think that they are genuine. She added that 'The Library of Congress and Lincoln scholars believe that any connection made between Lincoln and the "Ten Points" is spurious.'

You dirty rat!

Associated with the American film star James Cagney, who was particularly known for playing gangsters. However, the words were not used by him in any film. In a speech at the American Film Institute banquet, 13 March 1974, recorded in *Cagney by Cagney* (1976), he said: 'Frank Gorshin—oh, Frankie, just in passing: I never said "Mmm, you dirty rat!" What I actually did say was "Judy! Judy! Judy!"' (Cagney was referring to a line which, again apocryphally, was frequently attributed to Cary Grant.)

'You dirty rat!'

You have deliberately tasted two whole worms

William Archibald Spooner, who gave his name to the 'spoonerism', a verbal error in which a speaker accidentally transposes the initial sounds or letters of two or more words, has not unnaturally had a number of ingenious alterations attributed to him. One of the more notable of these, 'You have deliberately tasted two whole worms and you can leave Oxford by the town drain' appeared under this name in the second edition of the *Oxford Dictionary of Quotations*, published in 1953. (A longer version, printed in the 1948 *Oxford University What's What* ran 'You have tasted your worm, you have hissed my mystery lectures, and you must leave by the first town drain.') It was however omitted from the *Dictionary*'s third edition of 1979, with a note to the effect that many alleged 'Spoonerisms' were known to be apocryphal. (William Hayter's *Spooner*, published in 1977, had so categorized this particular example.)

You've never had it so good

A statement of political and economic prosperity, as in the following from a *Daily Telegraph* column of February 2001: 'Millbank's strategic response to all this will be to say that Tony Blair is responsible for Britain's economic prosperity: in short that 'you've never had it so good.'

The comment is widely attributed to Harold Macmillan in his 'Supermac' phase as successful Prime Minister. It derives from a rather longer passage, from a speech in July 1957, in which he set out very much the claim enshrined in the pithier line:

> Let us be frank about it: most of our people have never had it so good. Go around the country, go to the industrial towns, go to the farms, and you'll see a state of prosperity such as we have never had in my lifetime— nor indeed ever in the history of this country. What is beginning to worry some of us is 'Is it too good to be true?' or perhaps I should say 'Is it too good to last?'

Interestingly, the version which has become part of the common stock is very close to an American political slogan of a few years earlier. In 1952, Adlai Stevenson campaigned for the Democratic presidential nomination with the slogan '**You never had it so good**.'

Name Index

Acton, Lord (1834–1902), English historian
Power corrupts

Adams, John (1735–1826), American statesman, 2nd President
Facts are stupid things

Adams, John Quincy (1767–1848), American statesman, 6th President
One indissoluble bond

Adams, Samuel (1722–1803), American patriot
The British are coming!, What a glorious morning for America

Addison, Joseph (1672–1719), English poet and dramatist
He who hesitates is lost

Agar, Herbert (1897–1980), American poet and writer
The truth which makes one free

Alcuin (c.735–804), English scholar and theologian
Vox populi, vox humbug

Ambrose, St (c.339–97), bishop of Milan
When in Rome, do as the Romans do

Amery, Leo (1873–1955), British Conservative politician
Speak for England

Amherst, Lord (1773–1857), British diplomat
All we have done is awaken a sleeping giant

Amis, Kingsley (1922–95), English novelist and poet
Man's love is of man's life a thing apart, Outside every fat man

Andrewes, Lancelot (1555–1626), English bishop
A cold coming they had of it

Arbuthnot, John (d. 1735), British physician and satirist
Adding a new terror to life

Armstrong, Louis (1901–71), American singer and jazz musician
Man, if you gotta ask, you'll never know

Armstrong, Neil (1930–), American astronaut
One small step for man

Armstrong, Robert (1927–), British civil servant
Economical with the truth

Arnold, Matthew (1822–88), English poet and essayist
The battle of Waterloo was won on the playing fields of Eton, City of dreaming spires, Culture is the best that has been thought and said

Asquith, H. H. (1852–1928), British Liberal statesman
Germany is my spiritual home, Mr Balfour's poodle

Astaire, Fred (1899–1987), American dancer, singer, and actor
Backwards and in high heels

Attlee, Clement (1883–1967), British Labour statesman
An empty taxi, The voice we heard was that of Mr Churchill

Aristotle (384–322 BC), Greek philosopher
A beginning, a muddle, and an end

Auden, W. H. (1907–73), English poet
When he cried, the little children died

Augustine of Hippo, St (AD 354–430), Roman Christian theologian
Do what thou wilt, The good Christian should beware of mathematicians

Austen, Jane (1775–1817), English novelist
Safety in numbers

Heren, Louis (1919–95), English journalist
Why is this lying bastard lying to me?

Hildegard of Bingen (1098–1179), German abbess, scholar, and composer
A feather on the breath of God

Hillel the Elder (c.60BC–c.AD9), Jewish scholar and teacher
If we are not for ourselves, then who will be with us?

Hitchcock, Alfred (1889–1980), British-born American film director
Actors are cattle

Hogan, Paul (1939–), Australian actor
Throw another shrimp on the barbie

Holcroft, Thomas (1744–1809), English dramatist
Mind has no sex

Holmes, Oliver Wendell, Jr. (1841–1935), American Supreme Court Justice
Ask not what your country can do for you, Shouting fire in a crowded theatre

Hooker, Richard (c.1554–1600), English theologian and clergyman
An inn where all are received

Hoover, Herbert (1874–1964), American statesman, 31st President
A chicken in every pot

Horace (65–8 BC), Roman poet
Homer sometimes nods

Housman, A. E. (1859–1936), English poet
Justify the ways of God to man

Howard, Sidney, American screenwriter
Frankly, my dear, I don't give a damn

Hubbard, Elbert (1859–1915), American writer
Build a better mousetrap

Huxley, Aldous (1894–1963), English novelist
The proper study of mankind is books

Huxley, Thomas Henry (1825–95), English biologist
A little knowledge is a dangerous thing

Ingersoll, Robert G. (1833–99), American lawyer and orator
An honest God is the noblest work of man, Will it play in Peoria?

Jackson, 'Shoeless' Joe (1889–1951), American baseball player
If you build it, they will come

Jagger, Mick (1943–), British rock star
Who breaks a butterfly on a wheel?

James, Henry (1843–1916), American novelist and essayist
All human life is there

Jefferson, Thomas (1743–1826), American statesman, 3rd President
Dissent is the highest form of patriotism, Few die and none resign

Jenkins, Roy (1920–2003), British Labour politician
Mr Balfour's poodle

John (1165–1216), King of England
Justice delayed is justice denied

John of the Cross, St (1542–91), Spanish mystic and poet
Dark night of the soul

Johnson, Dorothy (1905–84), American writer
When the legend becomes fact, print the legend

Johnstone, John Benn (1803–91), English dramatist
Once aboard the lugger

Johst, Hans (1890–1978), German dramatist
Whenever I hear the word culture, I reach for my pistol

Josephine (1763–1814), Empress of the French
Not tonight, Josephine

Keats, John (1795–1821), English poet
A thing of beauty and a boy forever

Kelly, Walt (1913–73), American cartoonist
We have met the enemy, and he is us

Kelvin, Lord (1824–1907), British scientist
If you cannot measure it, then it is not science

Kennedy, John Fitzgerald (1917–63), American statesman, 35th President
Ask not what your country can do for you, Engineers of the soul

man challenges, You've never had it so good

Madison, James (1751–1836), American statesman, 4th President
Religion is the foundation of government

Magee, John Gillespie (1922–41), American airman
Slipped the surly bonds of earth to touch the face of God

Major, John (1943–), British Conservative statesman
Old maids biking to Holy Communion

Manilius (1st century AD), Roman poet
He snatched the lightning shaft from heaven

Marie Antoinette (1755–93), Queen of France
Let them eat cake

Marx, Karl (1818–83), German political philosopher
Nothing to lose but your yolks

Mather, Increase (1639–1723), American Puritan cleric and historian
A hundred guilty witches

Mawhinney, Brian (1940–), British Conservative politician
Tell your kids to get their scooters off my lawn

Maxton, James (1885–1946), British Labour politician
If you can't ride two horses at once

Mencken, H. L. (1880–1956), American journalist
Nobody ever lost money by underrating public taste

Millar, Ronald (1919–), British dramatist and speechwriter
The lady's not for turning

Millay, Edna St Vincent (1892–1950), American poet
Justice delayed is justice denied

Milton, John (1608–74), English poet
Fresh fields and pastures new, Justify the ways of God to man, Trip the light fantastic

Mitchell, John (1913–88), American lawyer
Watch what we do, not what we say

Mitchell, Margaret (1900–49), American novelist
Frankly, my dear, I don't give a damn

Moltke, Helmuth von (1800–91), Prussian military commander
No plan survives first contact with the enemy

Mondale, Walter (1928–), American Democratic politician
Where's the beef?

Montesquieu (1689–1755), French political philosopher
The sick man of —

Moore, Jo, British government adviser
A good day to bury bad news

Moore, Thomas (1779–1852), Irish musician and songwriter
I never loved a dear gazelle

Morgan, John A. Tyler (1824–1907), American politician
A lie is an abomination unto the Lord

Morton, Rogers (1914–79), American politician and presidential adviser
Rearrange the deckchairs on the Titanic

Morton, Thomas (c.1764–1838), English dramatist
Praise from Sir Hubert is praise indeed

Motley, John Lothrop (1814–77), American historian
When he cried, the little children died

Mussolini, Benito (1883–1945), Italian fascist dictator
Made the trains run on time

Nast, Thomas (1840–1902), German-born American cartoonist
What are you going to do about it?

Napoleon I (1769–1821), Emperor of the French
All we have done is awaken a sleeping giant, The English are a nation of shopkeepers, He once shot a publisher, Not tonight, Josephine

Simpson, O. J. (1947–), American football player
If the glove doesn't fit, you must acquit

Simpson, Tommy (1937–67), British cyclist
Put me back on my bike

Sitwell, Edith (1887–1964), English writer
Two wise acres and a cow

Sitwell, Osbert (1892–1969), English writer
Two wise acres and a cow

Sitwell, Sacheverell (1897–1988), English writer
Two wise acres and a cow

Smelt, Maurice, British journalist
All human life is there

Smith, Adam (1723–90), Scottish philosopher and economist
The English are a nation of shopkeepers

Smith, Sydney (1771–1845), English clergyman and essayist
Books do furnish a room

Somoza, Anastasio (1925–80), Nicaraguan dictator
It's not the voting that's democracy, it's the counting

Soule, John L. B. (1815–91), American journalist
Go west, young man

Spooner, William Archibald (1844–1930), English scholar
You have deliberately tasted two whole worms

Stalin, Joseph (1879–1953), Soviet statesman
Engineers of the soul, It's not the voting that's democracy, it's the counting

Stevenson, Adlai (1900–65), American Democratic politician
A heartbeat away from the Presidency, A lie is an abomination unto the Lord, Nothing to lose but your yolks, Rather light a candle than curse the darkness, You've never had it so good

Stoppard, Tom (1937–), Czech-born British dramatist
Comment is free, but facts are on expenses, It's not the voting that's democracy, it's the counting, Responsibility without power, Save the gerund, and screw the whale

Strachey, Lytton (1880–1932), English writer
The time was out of joint

Sutton, Willie (1901–80), American bank robber
I rob banks because that's where the money is

Swift, Jonathan (1667–1745), Irish poet and satirist
Adding a new terror to life

Talleyrand, Charles Maurice de (1754–1838), French statesman
Treason is a matter of dates

Tertullian (c.AD 160–c.240), early Christian theologian
See how these Christians love one another

Thatcher, Margaret (1925–), British Conservative stateswoman, Prime Minister
It's a funny old world, The lady's not for turning, Pennies don't fall from heaven, Rejoice, rejoice, Spend less time with one's family

Thaves, Bob, American cartoonist
Backwards and in high heels

Thornton, John Wingate (1818–78), American lawyer
One indissoluble bond

Thorpe, Jeremy (1929–), British Liberal politician
Greater love hath no man than this, that he lay down his friends for his life

Thurlow, Lord (1731–1806), English jurist and Lord Chancellor
Corporations have neither bodies to be punished

Turgot, Anne-Robert-Jacques (1727–81), French economist and politician
He snatched the lightning shaft from heaven

Twain, Mark (1835-1910), American writer
Economical with the truth, I am *the* American, Reports of my death have been greatly exaggerated

Tweed, William Magear 'Boss' (1823-78), American Democratic politician and Tammany leader
What are you going to do about it?

Virgil (70-19 BC), Roman poet
Rivers of blood

Voltaire (1694-1778), French writer and philosopher
I disapprove of what you say

Wallace, William Ross (d. 1881), American lawyer and poet
Instead of rocking the cradle

Walpole, Horace (1717-97), English writer and connoisseur
Sketch the ruins of St Paul's

Ward, Mrs Humphrey (1851-1920), English novelist
Germany is my spiritual home

Washington, George (1732-99), American statesman, 1st President
I had hoped that liberal and enlightened thought would have reconciled the Christians, It is impossible to rightly govern the world without God and the Bible

Weissmuller, Johnny (1904-84), American swimmer and film actor
Me Tarzan, you Jane

Welland, Colin (1934-), British actor and screenwriter
The British are coming!

Wellington, Duke of (1769-1862), British soldier and statesman
The battle of Waterloo was won on the playing fields of Eton, I don't know what effect these men will have upon the enemy

Wells, H. G. (1866-1946), English writer
The war to end war

West, Mae (1892-1980), American film actress
Is that a pistol in your pocket?, Why don't you come up and see me sometime?

Whitelocke, Bulstrode (1605-75), English parliamentarian
Take away these baubles

Wilde, Oscar (1854-1900), Irish dramatist and writer
England and America are two countries divided by a common language

Wilensky, Robert (1951-), American academic
Monkeys on typewriters

Wilhelm II (1859-1941), German Emperor
A contemptible little army

Wilson, Harold (1916-95), British Labour statesman
The pound in your pocket, Tell your kids to get their scooters off my lawn, A week is a long time in politics, The white heat of technology

Wilson, Woodrow (1856-1924), American Democratic statesman, 28th President
The war to end war

Wodehouse, P. G. (1881-1975), English writer
Elementary, my dear Watson

Wollstonecraft, Mary (1759-97), English feminist
Mind has no sex

Woodward, Robert (1943-), American journalist
Follow the money

Wordsworth, William (1770-1850), English poet
Power corrupts

Yamamoto, Isoruko (1884-1943), Japanese admiral
All we have done is awaken a sleeping giant

Zinn, Howard, American historian
Dissent is the highest form of patriotism